Extent, Nature, and Consequences of Intimate Partner Violence

Patricia Tjaden
Nancy Thoennes

Findings From the National Violence Against Women Survey

July 2000
NCJ 181867

U.S. Department of Justice
Office of Justice Programs
810 Seventh Street N.W.
Washington, DC 20531

Janet Reno
Attorney General

Daniel Marcus
Acting Associate Attorney General

Mary Lou Leary
Acting Assistant Attorney General

Julie E. Samuels
Acting Director, National Institute of Justice

Office of Justice Programs
World Wide Web Site
http://www.ojp.usdoj.gov

National Institute of Justice
World Wide Web Site
http://www.ojp.usdoj.gov/nij

CENTERS FOR DISEASE CONTROL
AND PREVENTION

Julie E. Samuels
Acting Director, National Institute of Justice

Stephen B. Thacker
Acting Director, National Center for Injury Prevention and Control

This research was sponsored jointly by the National Institute of Justice and the Centers for Disease Control and Prevention under NIJ Grant # 93–IJ–CX–0012. The opinions and conclusions expressed in this document are solely those of the authors and do not necessarily reflect the views of the U.S. Department of Justice or the Centers for Disease Control and Prevention.

The National Institute of Justice is a component of the Office of Justice Programs, which also includes the Bureau of Justice Assistance, the Bureau of Justice Statistics, the Office of Juvenile Justice and Delinquency Prevention, and the Office for Victims of Crime.

Executive Summary

This report presents findings from the National Violence Against Women (NVAW) Survey on the extent, nature, and consequences of intimate partner violence in the United States. The National Institute of Justice and the Centers for Disease Control and Prevention cosponsored the survey through a grant to the Center for Policy Research. The survey consists of telephone interviews with a nationally representative sample of 8,000 U.S. women and 8,000 U.S. men about their experiences as victims of various forms of violence, including intimate partner violence.

The survey compares intimate partner victimization rates among women and men, specific racial groups, Hispanics and non-Hispanics, and same-sex and opposite-sex cohabitants. It also examines risk factors associated with intimate partner violence, the rate of injury among rape and physical assault victims, injured victims' use of medical services, and victims' involvement with the justice system.

Analysis of the survey data produced the following results:

- Intimate partner violence is pervasive in U.S. society. Nearly 25 percent of surveyed women and 7.6 percent of surveyed men said they were raped and/or physically assaulted by a current or former spouse, cohabiting partner, or date at some time in their lifetime; 1.5 percent of surveyed women and 0.9 percent of surveyed men said they were raped and/or physically assaulted by a partner in the previous 12 months. According to these estimates, approximately 1.5 million women and 834,732 men are raped and/or physically assaulted by an intimate partner annually in the United States. Because many victims are

victimized more than once, the number of intimate partner victimizations exceeds the number of intimate partner victims annually. Thus, approximately 4.8 million intimate partner rapes and physical assaults are perpetrated against U.S. women annually, and approximately 2.9 million intimate partner physical assaults are committed against U.S. men annually. These findings suggest that intimate partner violence is a serious criminal justice and public health concern.

- Stalking by intimates is more prevalent than previously thought. Almost 5 percent of surveyed women and 0.6 percent of surveyed men reported being stalked by a current or former spouse, cohabiting partner, or date at some time in their lifetime; 0.5 percent of surveyed women and 0.2 percent of surveyed men reported being stalked by such a partner in the previous 12 months. According to these estimates, 503,485 women and 185,496 men are stalked by an intimate partner annually in the United States. These estimates exceed previous nonscientific "guesstimates" of stalking prevalence in the general population. These findings suggest that intimate partner stalking is a serious criminal justice problem, and States should continue to develop constitutionally sound and effective antistalking statutes and intervention strategies.

- Women experience more intimate partner violence than do men. The NVAW survey found that women are significantly more likely than men to report being victims of intimate partner violence whether it is rape, physical assault, or stalking and whether the timeframe is the person's lifetime or the previous 12 months. These findings support data from the Bureau of Justice Statistics' National Crime Victimization Survey, which consistently show women are at significantly greater risk of intimate partner violence than are men. However, they contradict data from the National Family Violence Survey, which consistently show men and women are equally likely to be physically assaulted by an intimate partner. Studies are needed to determine how different survey methodologies affect women's and men's responses to questions about intimate partner violence.

- Rates of intimate partner violence vary significantly among women of diverse racial backgrounds. The survey found that Asian/Pacific Islander women and men tend to report lower rates of intimate partner violence than do women and men from other minority backgrounds, and African-American and American Indian/Alaska Native women and men report higher rates. However, differences among minority groups diminish when other sociodemographic and relationship variables are controlled. More research is needed to determine how much of the difference in intimate partner prevalence rates among women and men of different racial and ethnic backgrounds can be explained by the respondent's willingness to disclose intimate partner violence and how much by social, demographic, and environmental factors. Research is also needed to determine how prevalence rates vary among women and men of diverse American Indian/Alaska Native and Asian/Pacific Islander groups.

- Violence perpetrated against women by intimates is often accompanied by emotionally abusive and controlling behavior. The survey found that women whose partners were jealous, controlling, or verbally abusive were significantly more likely to report being raped, physically assaulted, and/or

stalked by their partners, even when other sociodemographic and relationship characteristics were controlled. Indeed, having a verbally abusive partner was the variable most likely to predict that a woman would be victimized by an intimate partner. These findings support the theory that violence perpetrated against women by intimates is often part of a systematic pattern of dominance and control.

- Women experience more chronic and injurious physical assaults at the hands of intimate partners than do men. The survey found that women who were physically assaulted by an intimate partner averaged 6.9 physical assaults by the same partner, but men averaged 4.4 assaults. The survey also found that 41.5 percent of the women who were physically assaulted by an intimate partner were injured during their most recent assault, compared with 19.9 percent of the men. These findings suggest that research aimed at understanding and preventing intimate partner violence against women should be stressed.

- Women living with female intimate partners experience less intimate partner violence than women living with male intimate partners. Slightly more than 11 percent of the women who had lived with a woman as part of a couple reported being raped, physically assaulted, and/or stalked by a female cohabitant, but 30.4 percent of the women who had married or lived with a man as part of a couple reported such violence by a husband or male cohabitant. These findings suggest that lesbian couples experience less intimate partner violence than do heterosexual couples; however, more research is needed to support or refute this conclusion.

- Men living with male intimate partners experience more intimate partner violence than do men who live with female intimate partners. Approximately 15 percent of the men who had lived with a man as a couple reported being raped, physically assaulted, and/or stalked by a male cohabitant, while 7.7 percent of the men who had married or lived with a woman as a couple reported such violence by a wife or female cohabitant. These findings, combined with those presented in the previous bullet, provide further evidence that intimate partner violence is perpetrated primarily by men, whether against male or female intimates. Thus, strategies for preventing intimate partner violence should focus on risks posed by men.

- The U.S. medical community treats millions of intimate partner rapes and physical assaults annually. Of the estimated 4.8 million intimate partner rapes and physical assaults perpetrated against women annually, approximately 2 million will result in an injury to the victim, and 552,192 will result in some type of medical treatment to the victim. Of the estimated 2.9 million intimate partner physical assaults perpetrated against men annually, 581,391 will result in an injury to the victim, and 124,999 will result in some type of medical treatment to the victim. Many medically treated victims receive multiple forms of care (e.g., ambulance services, emergency room care, or physical therapy) and multiple treatments (e.g., several days in the hospital) for the same victimization. Therefore, the number of medical personnel treating injuries annually is in the millions. To better meet the needs of intimate partner violence victims, medical professionals should receive training on the physical consequences of intimate partner violence and appropriate medical intervention strategies.

- Most intimate partner victimizations are not reported to the police. Approximately one-fifth of all rapes, one-quarter of all physical assaults, and one-half of all stalkings perpetrated against female respondents by intimates were reported to the police. Even fewer rapes, physical assaults, and stalkings perpetrated against male respondents by intimates were reported. The majority of victims who did not report their victimization to the police thought the police would not or could not do anything on their behalf. These findings suggest that most victims of intimate partner violence do not consider the justice system an appropriate vehicle for resolving conflicts with intimates.

Acknowledgments

The authors thank staff at both the National Institute of Justice (NIJ) and the Centers for Disease Control and Prevention (CDC), in particular Lois Mock at NIJ and Linda Saltzman at CDC, for their advice and support in conducting the research.

The authors also thank Marcie-jo Kresnow, mathematical statistician at CDC, and anonymous NIJ peer reviewers for their thorough review and helpful comments on drafts of this report. Finally, the authors thank Christine Allison and Gay Dizinski at the Center for Policy Research for their help in producing and scrutinizing drafts of the report.

Contents

Exhibits

Introduction

Research on intimate partner violence has increased dramatically over the past 20 years. While greatly enhancing public awareness and understanding of this serious social problem, this research has also created much controversy and confusion. Findings of intimate partner victimization vary widely from study to study.[1] Some studies conclude that women and men are equally likely to be victimized by their partners,[2] but others conclude that women are more likely to be victimized.[3] Some studies conclude that minorities and whites suffer equal rates of intimate partner violence,[4] and others conclude that minorities suffer higher rates.[5]

In addition, there are many gaps in the scientific literature on intimate partner violence, such as the level of violence committed against men and women by same-sex intimates.[6] Little empirical data exist on the relationship between different forms of intimate partner violence, such as emotional abuse and physical assault.[7] Finally, little is known of the consequences of intimate partner violence, including rate of injury and victims' use of medical and justice system services.[8]

This Research Report addresses these and other issues related to intimate partner violence. The information presented in this report is based on findings from the National Violence Against Women (NVAW) Survey, a national telephone survey jointly sponsored by the National Institute of Justice (NIJ) and the Centers for Disease Control and Prevention (CDC). The survey, which was conducted from November 1995 to May 1996, consists of telephone interviews with a representative sample of 8,000 U.S. women and 8,000 U.S. men. Survey respondents were queried about their experiences as victims of various forms of violence, including rape, physical assault, and stalking by intimate partners. Victimized respondents were asked detailed questions about the characteristics and consequences of their victimization, including the extent and nature of any injuries they sustained, their use of medical services, and their involvement with the justice system.

This Research Report also summarizes the survey's findings on victimization rates among women and men, specific racial groups, Hispanics and non-Hispanics, and opposite-sex and same-sex cohabitants. It examines risk factors associated with intimate partner violence, rates of injury among rape and physical assault victims, injured victims' use of medical services, and victims' involvement with the justice system. Although this report focuses on women's and men's experiences as victims of intimate partner violence, complete details about men's and women's experiences as victims of rape, physical assault, and stalking by all types of assailants are contained in earlier NIJ and CDC reports (see sidebar, "Other Publications in the Series").

Because of the sensitive nature of the survey, state-of-the-art techniques were used to protect the confidentiality of the information being sought and to minimize the potential for retraumatizing victims of violence and jeopardizing the safety of respondents.

• The sample was generated through random-digit dialing, thereby ensuring that only a 10-digit telephone number linked the respondent to the survey. The area code and telephone exchanges were included as part of the completed interview for each case in the dataset for analysis purposes, but the last four digits of the telephone number were eliminated.

Other Publications in the Series

Other publications related to the National Violence Against Women Survey include:

- *Stalking in America: Findings From the National Violence Against Women Survey,* Research in Brief, by Patricia Tjaden and Nancy Thoennes, Washington, D.C.: U.S. Department of Justice, National Institute of Justice, 1998, NCJ 169592.

- *Prevalence, Incidence, and Consequences of Violence Against Women: Findings From the National Violence Against Women Survey,* Research in Brief, by Patricia Tjaden and Nancy Thoennes, Washington, D.C.: U.S. Department of Justice, National Institute of Justice, 1998, NCJ 172837.

- *Prevalence, Incidence, and Consequences of Violence Against Women,* Research Report, by Patricia Tjaden and Nancy Thoennes, Washington, D.C.: U.S. Department of Justice, National Institute of Justice, forthcoming.

To obtain copies of these documents, visit NIJ's Web site at http://www.ojp.usdoj.gov/nij or contact the National Criminal Justice Service at P.O. Box 6000, Rockville, MD 20849–6000, 800–851–3420 or 301–519–5500, or send an e-mail message to *askncjrs@ncjrs.org.* Additional reports in the series are forthcoming.

Also of interest:

- *National Violence Against Women Methodology Report* by Patricia Tjaden, Steven Leadbetter, John Boyle, and Robert A. Bardwell, Atlanta: Centers for Disease Control and Prevention, National Center for Injury Prevention and Control, forthcoming.

Learn about the availability of this report and other CDC family and intimate violence prevention activities by visiting the National Center for Injury Prevention and Control's Web site at *http://www.cdc.gov/ncipc/dvp/fivpt.*

- The survey introduction informed respondents that their answers would be kept confidential and that participation in the survey was voluntary.

- Respondents were given a toll-free number to call to verify the authenticity of the survey or to respond to the survey at a later date. Respondents also were told to use this number should they need to hang up suddenly during the interview.

- Only female interviewers interviewed female respondents. (To measure the possible effects of interviewer gender on male responses to survey questions, half of the male respondents were interviewed by male interviewers and half by female interviewers.)

- Interviewers were instructed to schedule a callback interview if they thought someone was listening to the interview on another line or was in the room with the respondent.

- Interviewers, out of concern that the interview might cause some victims of violence to experience emotional trauma, were provided with rape crisis and domestic violence hotline telephone numbers from around the country. If a respondent showed signs of distress, he or she was provided with an appropriate hotline referral.

In addition to lessening the possibility that respondents might be harmed due to their participation in the survey, these techniques improved the quality of the information gathered.

Notes

1. For example, lifetime rates of victimization by an intimate range from 9 to 30 percent for women and from 13 to 16 percent for men. See Nisonoff, L., and I. Bittman, "Spouse Abuse: Incidence and Relationship to Selected Demographic Variables," *Victimology* 4 (1979): 131–140; Peterson, R., "Social Class, Social Learning, and Wife Abuse," *Social Service Review* 50 (1980): 390–406; Schulman, M., *A Survey of Spousal Violence Against Women In Kentucky,* Study Number 792701, Washington, D.C.: U.S. Department of Justice, Law Enforcement Assistance Administration, 1979; Teske, R.H.C., and M.L. Parker, *Spouse Abuse in Texas: A Study of Women's Attitudes and Experiences,* Newark, New Jersey: Criminal Justice/National Center for Crime and Delinquency, John Cotton Dana Library, 1983; Scanzoni, J., *Sex Roles, Women's Work, and Marital Conflict,* Lexington, Massachusetts: Lexington Books, 1978.

2. Schafer, J., R. Caetano, C.L. Clark, "Rates of Intimate Partner Violence in the United States," *American Journal of Public Health* 88 (11) (1998): 1702–1704; Straus, M.A., "Trends in Cultural Norms and Rates of Partner Violence: An Update to 1992," in *Understanding Partner Violence: Prevalence, Causes, Consequences, and Solutions,* Families in Focus Series, eds. M.A. Straus and S.M. Smith, Minneapolis: National Council on Family Relations, 1995: 30–33; Straus, M., and R. Gelles, "Societal Change and Change in Family Violence From 1975 to 1985 as Revealed by Two National Surveys," *Journal of Marriage and the Family* 48 (1987): 465–479.

3. Bachman, R., *Violence Against Women: A National Crime Victimization Survey Report*, Washington, D.C.: U.S. Department of Justice, Bureau of Justice Statistics, 1994, NCJ 145325; Bachman, R., and L.E. Saltzman, *Violence Against Women: Estimates From the Redesigned Survey,* Special Report, Washington, D.C.: U.S. Department of Justice, Bureau of Justice Statistics, 1995, NCJ 154348; Gaquin, D., "Spouse Abuse: Data from the National Crime Survey," *Victimology* 2 (1977–78): 634–643; Greenfeld, L., M.R. Rand, D. Craven, P.A. Klaus, C.A. Perkins, C. Ringel, G. Warchol, C. Matson, and J.A. Fox, *Violence by Intimates: Analysis of Data on Crimes by Current or Former Spouses, Boyfriends, and Girlfriends*, Bureau of Justice Statistics Factbook, Washington, D.C.: U.S. Department of Justice, Bureau of Justice Statistics, 1998, NCJ 167237; Klaus, P., and M. Rand, *Family Violence*, Special Report, Washington, D.C.: U.S. Department of Justice, Bureau of Justice Statistics, 1984, NCJ 093449.

4. Bachman, *Violence Against Women: A National Crime Victimization Survey Report.*

5. For example, see Bachman, R., *Death and Violence on the Reservation: Homicide, Family Violence, and Suicide in American Indian Populations*, Westport, Connecticut: Auburn House, 1992; Cazenave, N.A., and M.A. Straus, "Race, Class, Network Embeddedness and Family Violence: A Search for Potent Support Systems," *Journal of Comparative Family Studies* 10 (3) (1979): 281–300; Gelles, R., "Violence in the Family: A Review of Research in the Seventies," *Journal of Marriage and the Family* 42 (1980): 873–885; Hampton, R.L., "Family Violence and Homicides in the Black Community: Are They Linked?" in *Violence in the Black Family: Correlates and Consequences*, ed. R.L. Hampton, Lexington, Massachusetts, 1987: 135–187; Neff, J.A., B. Holamon, and T.D. Schluter, "Spousal Violence Among Anglos, Blacks, and Mexican Americans: The Role of Demographic Variables, Psychological Predictors, and Alcohol Consumption," *Journal of Family Violence* 10 (1) (1995): 1–21; Shoemaker, D.J., and J.S. Williams, "The Subculture of Violence and Ethnicity," *Journal of Criminal Justice* 15 (6) (1987): 461–472; and *Behind Closed Doors*, ed. Straus, M.A., R.J. Gelles, and S. Steinmetz, Newbury Park, California: Sage Publications, 1980.

6. Renzetti, C.M., "Violence and Abuse Among Same-Sex Couples," in *Violence Between Intimate Partners: Patterns, Causes, and Effects,* ed. Cardarelli, A.P., Boston: Allyn and Bacon, 1997: 70–89.

7. National Research Council, *Understanding Violence Against Women,* Washington, D.C.: National Academy Press, 1996: 4–5.

8. *Ibid.*

Defining Intimate Partner Violence

There is currently little consensus among researchers on exactly how to define the term "intimate partner violence."[1] As a result, definitions of the term vary widely from study to study, making comparisons difficult. One source of controversy revolves around whether to limit the definition of the term to acts carried out with the intention of, or perceived intention of, causing physical pain or injury to another person. Although this approach presents a narrow definition of intimate partner violence that can be readily operationalized, it ignores the myriad behaviors that persons may use to control, intimidate, and otherwise dominate another person in the context of an intimate relationship. These behaviors may include acts such as verbal abuse, imprisonment, humiliation, stalking, and denial of access to financial resources, shelter, or services.

Another source of controversy revolves around whether to limit the definition of the term to violence occurring between persons who are married or living together as a couple or to include persons who are dating or who consider themselves a couple but live in separate domiciles. At present the research literature is bifurcated, with some studies focusing on violence occurring in marital or heterosexual cohabiting relationships and others focusing on violence occurring in heterosexual dating relationships. Only a handful of studies examine violence in same-sex cohabiting or dating relationships.

The definition of intimate partner violence used in the NVAW Survey includes rape, physical assault, and stalking perpetrated by current and former dates, spouses, and cohabiting partners, with cohabiting meaning living together at least some of the time as a couple. Both same-sex and opposite-sex cohabitants are included in the definition. The survey's definition of intimate partner violence resembles the one developed by CDC[2] because it includes violence occurring between persons who have a current or former dating, marital, or cohabiting relationship and same-sex and opposite-sex cohabitants. However, it deviates from CDC's definition because it includes stalking as well as rape and physical assault.

For purposes of the survey, "rape" is defined as an event that occurs without the victim's consent and involves the use of threat or force to penetrate the victim's vagina or anus by penis, tongue, fingers, or object or the victim's mouth by penis. The definition includes both attempted and completed rape. "Physical assault" is defined as behaviors that threaten, attempt, or actually inflict physical harm. The definition includes a wide range of behaviors, from slapping, pushing, and shoving to using a gun. "Stalking" is defined as a course of conduct directed at a specific person involving repeated visual or physical proximity; nonconsensual communication; verbal, written, or implied threats; or a combination thereof that would cause fear in a reasonable person, with "repeated" meaning on two or more occasions. The definition of stalking used in the survey does not require stalkers to make a credible threat against victims, but it does require victims to feel a high level of fear. The specific questions used to screen respondents for rape, physical assault, and stalking victimization are behaviorally specific and are designed to leave little doubt in the respondent's mind as to what is being measured (see sidebar, "Survey Screening Questions").

Survey Screening Questions

Rape: Five questions were used to screen respondents for completed and attempted rape victimization:[a]

- [Female respondents only] *Has a man or boy ever made you have sex by using force or threatening to harm you or someone close to you? Just so there is no mistake, by sex we mean putting his penis in your vagina.*

- *Has anyone, male or female, ever made you have oral sex by using force or threat of force? Just so there is no mistake, by oral sex we mean that a man or boy put his penis in your mouth or someone, male or female, penetrated your vagina or anus with their mouth.*

- *Has anyone ever made you have anal sex by using force or threat of force? Just so there is no mistake, by anal sex we mean that a man or boy put his penis in your anus.*

- *Has anyone, male or female, ever put fingers or objects in your vagina or anus against your will or by using force or threats?*

- *Has anyone, male or female, ever **attempted** to make you have vaginal, oral, or anal sex against your will but intercourse or penetration did not occur?*

Physical assault: A modified version of the original Conflict Tactics Scale was used to screen respondents for physical assault they experienced as an adult at the hands of another adult:[b]

- *Not counting any incidents you have already mentioned, after you became an adult, did any other adult, male or female, ever:*

  — *Throw something at you that could hurt?*

  — *Push, grab, or shove you?*

  — *Pull your hair?*

  — *Slap or hit you?*

  — *Kick or bite you?*

  — *Choke or attempt to drown you?*

  — *Hit you with some object?*

  — *Beat you up?*

  — *Threaten you with a gun?*

  — *Threaten you with a knife or other weapon?*

  — *Use a gun on you?*

  — *Use a knife or other weapon on you?*

Stalking: The following questions were used to screen respondents for stalking victimization:

- *Not including bill collectors, telephone solicitors, or other salespeople, has anyone, male or female, ever:*

  — *Followed or spied on you?*

  — *Sent you unsolicited letters or written correspondence?*

  — *Made unsolicited phone calls to you?*

  — *Stood outside your home, school, or workplace?*

  — *Showed up at places you were even though he or she had no business being there?*

  — *Left unwanted items for you to find?*

  — *Tried to communicate in other ways against your will?*

  — *Vandalized your property or destroyed something you loved?*

Respondents who answered *yes* to one or more of these questions were asked whether anyone had ever done any of these things on more than one occasion and whether they felt frightened or feared bodily harm as a result of these behaviors. Only respondents who reported being victimized on more than one occasion and who were very frightened or feared bodily harm were counted as stalking victims.

Victim-perpetrator relationship: Respondents who answered affirmatively to the rape, physical assault, and/or stalking screening questions were asked whether their attacker was a current or ex-spouse, a male live-in partner, a female live-in partner, a relative, someone else they knew, or a stranger. Respondents disclosing victimization by an ex-spouse or cohabiting partner were asked to further identify which spouse/partner victimized them (e.g., first ex-husband, current male live-in partner). Respondents disclosing victimization by a relative were asked to further

specify which relative victimized them (e.g., father, brother, uncle, cousin). Finally, respondents disclosing victimization by someone else they knew were asked to further specify the relationship they had with this person (e.g., date, boss, teacher, neighbor). Only victimizations perpetrated by current and former spouses, same-sex and opposite-sex cohabiting partners, and dates are included in the analyses discussed in this report.

a. Rape screening questions were adapted from those used in The National Women's Study, *Rape in America: A Report to the Nation,* National Victim Center and the Crime Victims Research and Treatment Center, Arlington, Virginia, April 23, 1992: 15.

b. Straus, M., "Measuring Intrafamily Conflict and Violence: The Conflict Tactics (CT) Scale," *Journal of Marriage and the Family* 41 (1979): 75–88.

Notes

1. National Research Council, *Understanding Violence Against Women,* Washington, D.C.: National Academy Press, 1996: 9–10.

2. Saltzman, L.E., J.L. Fanslow, P.M. McMahon, and G.A. Shelley, *Intimate Partner Violence Surveillance: Uniform Definitions and Recommended Data Elements,* Atlanta: National Center for Injury Prevention and Control, Centers for Disease Control and Prevention, 1999.

Prevalence and Incidence of Intimate Partner Violence

The NVAW Survey generated information on both the prevalence and incidence of intimate partner violence. "Prevalence" refers to the percentage of persons within a demographic group (e.g., female or male) who are victimized during a specific period, such as the person's lifetime or the previous 12 months. "Incidence" refers to the number of separate victimizations or incidents of violence committed against persons within a demographic group during a specific period. Incidence can also be expressed as a victimization rate, which is obtained by dividing the number of victimizations committed against persons in a demographic group by the number of persons in that demographic group and setting the rate to a standard population base, such as 1,000 persons.[1]

Intimate partner rape

Using a definition of rape that includes completed or attempted forced vaginal, oral, and anal sex, the survey found 7.7 percent of

Exhibit 1. Persons Victimized by an Intimate Partner in Lifetime and in Previous 12 Months, by Type of Victimization and Gender				
	In Lifetime			
	Percent		Number[a]	
Type of Victimization	Women (*n* = 8,000)	Men (*n* = 8,000)	Women (100,697,000)	Men (92,748,000)
Rape[b***]	7.7	0.3	7,753,669	278,244
Physical assault[b***]	22.1	7.4	22,254,037	6,863,352
Rape and/or physical assault[b***]	24.8	7.6	24,972,856	7,048,848
Stalking[b***]	4.8	0.6	4,833,456	556,488
Total victimized[b***]	25.5	7.9	25,677,735	7,327,092
	In Previous 12 Months			
	Percent		Number[a]	
Type of Violence	Women (*n* = 8,000)	Men (*n* = 8,000)	Women (100,697,000)	Men (92,748,000)
Rape	0.2	—[c]	201,394	—[c]
Physical assault[b*]	1.3	0.9	1,309,061	834,732
Rape and/or physical assault[b*]	1.5	0.9[d]	1,510,455	834,732
Stalking[b**]	0.5	0.2	503,485	185,496
Total victimized[b***]	1.8	1.1	1,812,546	1,020,228

[a] Based on estimates of women and men 18 years of age and older: Wetrogen, S.I., *Projections of the Population of States by Age, Sex, and Race: 1988 to 2010*, Current Population Reports, Washington, D.C.: U.S. Bureau of the Census, 1988: 25–1017.

[b] Differences between women and men are statistically significant: χ^2, $*p \leq .05$, $**p \leq .01$, $***p \leq .001$.

[c] Estimates not calculated on fewer than five victims.

[d] Because only three men reported being raped by an intimate partner in the previous 12 months, the percentage of men physically assaulted and physically assaulted and/or raped is the same.

Exhibit 2. Number of Rape, Physical Assault, and Stalking Victimizations Perpetrated by Intimate Partners Annually, by Victim Gender				
Type of Victimization	Number of Victims	Average Number of Victimizations per Victim[a]	Total Number of Victimizations	Annual Rate of Victimization per 1,000 Persons
Women				
Rape[c]	201,394	1.6[b]	322,230[b]	3.2
Physical assault	1,309,061	3.4	4,450,807	44.2
Stalking	503,485	1.0	503,485	5.0
Men				
Rape[c]	—	—	—	—
Physical assault	834,732	3.5	2,921,562	31.5
Stalking	185,496	1.0	185,496	1.8

[a]The standard error of the mean is 0.5 for female rape victims, 0.6 for female physical assault victims, and 0.6 for male physical assault victims. Because stalking by definition means repeated acts and because no victim was stalked by more than one perpetrator in the 12 months preceding the survey, the number of stalking victimizations was imputed to be the same as the number of stalking victims. Thus, the average number of stalking victimizations per victim is 1.0.

[b]Relative standard error exceeds 30 percent.

[c]Estimates not calculated on fewer than five victims.

surveyed women and 0.3 percent of surveyed men reported being raped by a current or former intimate partner at some time in their lifetime, and 0.2 percent ($n = 16$) of surveyed women reported being raped by a partner in the 12 months preceding the survey. Based on U.S. Census estimates of the number of women aged 18 years and older in the country, an estimated 201,394 women were forcibly raped by an intimate partner in the 12 months preceding the survey (exhibit 1). [The number of male rape victims ($n < 5$) was insufficient to reliably calculate annual prevalence estimates for men.]

Because women raped by an intimate partner in the previous 12 months averaged 1.6 rapes, the incidence of intimate partner rape (number of separate victimizations) exceeded the prevalence of intimate partner rape (number of victims). Thus, there were an estimated 322,230 intimate partner rapes committed against U.S. women during the 12 months preceding the survey. (This national estimate is based on only 16 women who reported being raped by an intimate partner in the previous 12 months and should be viewed with caution.) This figure equates to an annual victimization rate of 3.2 intimate partner rapes per 1,000 U.S. women aged 18 years and older ($322,230 \div 100,697,000 = 0.0032 \times 1,000 = 3.2$) (exhibit 2).

Intimate partner physical assault

Using a definition of physical assault that includes a range of behaviors, from slapping and hitting to using a gun, the survey found that 22.1 percent of surveyed women and 7.4 percent of surveyed men reported being physically assaulted by a current or former intimate partner at some time in their lifetime, whereas 1.3 percent of all surveyed women and 0.9 percent of all surveyed men reported being physically assaulted by such a partner in the previous 12 months. Thus, approximately 1.3 million women and 834,732 men were physically assaulted by an intimate partner in the 12 months preceding the survey (exhibit 1).

Because women and men who were physically assaulted by an intimate partner in the previous 12 months averaged 3.4 and 3.5 physical assaults, respectively, there were approximately 4.5 million intimate partner physical assaults perpetrated against women and approximately 2.9 million intimate partner physical assaults perpetrated against men in the 12 months preceding the survey. These figures equate to an annual victimization rate of 44.2 intimate partner physical assaults per 1,000 U.S. women aged 18 years and older ($4,450,807 \div 100,697,000 = 0.0442 \times 1,000 = 44.2$) and 31.5 intimate partner physical assaults per 1,000 U.S. men aged 18 years and older $(2,921,562 \div 92,748,000 = 0.0315 \times 1,000 = 31.5)$ (exhibit 2).

Results from the survey show that most physical assaults committed against women and men by intimates are relatively minor and consist of pushing, grabbing, shoving, slapping, and hitting. Fewer women and men reported that an intimate threw something that could hurt them, pulled their hair, kicked or beat them, or threatened them with a knife or gun. Only a negligible number reported that an intimate actually used a knife or gun on them (exhibit 3).

Intimate partner stalking

Using a definition of stalking that requires victims to feel a high level of fear, the survey found that 4.8 percent of surveyed women and 0.6 percent of surveyed men reported being stalked by a current or former intimate partner at some time in their lifetime; 0.5 percent of surveyed women and 0.2 percent of surveyed men reported being stalked by such a partner in the 12 months preceding the survey. These figures equate to an estimated 503,485 women and 185,496 men

who were stalked by an intimate partner in the 12 months preceding the survey (exhibit 1).

Because stalking by definition involves repeated acts of harassment and intimidation and because no respondent reported being stalked by more than one intimate in the 12 months preceding the survey, the incidence of intimate partner stalking is equivalent to the prevalence of intimate partner stalking. Thus, there were an estimated 503,485 stalking victimizations perpetrated against women and 185,496 stalking victimizations perpetrated against men by intimates in the year preceding the survey (exhibit 2). These figures equate to an annual victimization rate of 5 intimate partner stalkings per 1,000 U.S. women aged 18 years and older $(503,485 \div 100,697,000 = 0.005 \times 1,000 = 5.0)$ and 1.8 intimate partner stalkings per 1,000 U.S. men aged 18 years and older $(185,496 \div 97,748,000 = 0.0018 \times 1,000 = 1.8)$ (exhibit 2).

Note

1. Koss, M.P., and M.R. Harvey, *The Rape Victim: Clinical and Community Interventions,* 2d ed. Newbury Park, California: Sage Publications, 1991: 8–9.

Exhibit 3. Persons Physically Assaulted by an Intimate Partner in Lifetime, by Type of Assault and Victim Gender

Type of assault[a]	Women (%) (n = 8,000)	Men (%) (n = 8,000)
Threw something that could hurt	8.1	4.4
Pushed, grabbed, shoved	18.1	5.4
Pulled hair	9.1	2.3
Slapped, hit	16.0	5.5
Kicked, bit	5.5	2.6
Choked, tried to drown	6.1	0.5
Hit with object	5.0	3.2
Beat up	8.5	0.6
Threatened with gun	3.5	0.4
Threatened with knife	2.8	1.6
Used gun	0.7	0.1[b]
Used knife	0.9	0.8
Total reporting physical assault by intimate partner	**22.1**	**7.4**

[a]With the exception of "used gun" and "used knife," differences between women and men are statistically significant: χ^2, $p \leq .001$.
[b]Relative standard error exceeds 30 percent; statistical tests not performed.

Comparison With Previous Estimates

Intimate partner rape

No previous national survey has generated estimates of the lifetime prevalence of intimate partner rape.[1] However, a study of 930 women in San Francisco found that 8 percent were survivors of marital rape,[2] and a study of 323 ever-married/cohabited women in Boston found that 10 percent were survivors of wife or partner rape.[3] Though not directly comparable, the NVAW Survey finding that 7.7 percent of U.S. women have been raped by an intimate partner at some time in their lifetime is similar to these earlier community-based estimates.

The Bureau of Justice Statistics' National Crime Victimization Survey (NCVS), which is administered yearly, generates annual rape and sexual assault victimization estimates for women and men. One study based on 1992–93 NCVS data found that the average annual rate of rape and sexual assault by an intimate was 1.0 per 1,000 women aged 12 years and older.[4] This estimate is lower than the average annual rate of intimate partner rape for women generated by the NVAW Survey, which is 3.2 per 1,000 women aged 18 years and older (exhibit 2). However, direct comparisons between the findings of the two surveys are difficult to make because estimates reported by the two surveys refer to somewhat different populations and sexual victimizations, and the two surveys differ substantially methodologically (see "Deciphering Disparities in Survey Findings").

Intimate partner physical assault

Several community-based studies have generated estimates of the lifetime prevalence of physical assault by an intimate. Estimates from these surveys range from 9 to 30 percent for women and from 13 to 16 percent for men (see

note 1 in "Introduction"). In addition, a 1997 Gallup poll, which surveyed a nationally representative sample of 434 women and 438 men, found that 22 percent of women and 8 percent of men have been physically abused by a spouse or companion.[5] NVAW Survey estimates that 22.1 percent of women and 7.4 percent of men have been physically assaulted by an intimate at some time in their lifetime are nearly identical to the Gallup estimates.

National estimates of the *annual* rate of physical assault by an intimate come from two primary sources—the previously mentioned NCVS and the National Family Violence Survey (NFVS), which was first conducted in 1975 and then repeated in 1985. Portions of the NFVS were also included in the 1992 National Alcohol and Family Violence Survey and a special component of the 1995 National Alcohol Survey.

Annual rates of physical assault by an intimate generated from the NVAW Survey are substantially higher than those generated by the NCVS. One study based on 1992–93 NCVS data found that the average annual rate of simple and aggravated assault by an intimate was 7.6 per 1,000 women aged 12 years and older and 1.3 per 1,000 men aged 12 years and older.[6] A more recent study that used 1996 NCVS data and Federal Bureau of Investigation Uniform Crime Report homicide data—and combined data on intimate partner murder, rape, sexual assault, robbery, aggravated assault, and simple assault—found the annual rate of violent victimization by an intimate was 7.5 per 1,000 women aged 12 years and older and 1.4 per 1,000 men aged 12 years and older.[7] In comparison, the NVAW Survey annual rate of physical assault by an intimate was 44.2 per 1,000 women aged 18 years and older and 31.5 per 1,000 men aged 18 years and older. Thus, the

NVAW Survey annual rate of physical assault by an intimate far exceeds the NCVS annual rate of violent victimization by an intimate.

On the other hand, annual rates of physical assault generated from the NVAW Survey are substantially lower than those generated by the NFVS. The 1975 and 1985 NFVS found that 11 to 12 percent of married/cohabiting women and 12 percent of married/cohabiting men were physically assaulted by their intimate partner annually.[8] The 1992 National Alcohol and Family Violence Survey found that approximately 1.9 percent of married/cohabiting women were severely assaulted by a male partner annually, and approximately 4.5 percent of married/cohabiting men were severely assaulted by a female partner annually.[9] The 1995 National Alcohol Survey found that 5.2 to 13.6 percent of married/cohabiting couples experienced male-to-female partner violence, and 6.2 to 18.2 percent of married/cohabiting couples experienced female-to-male intimate partner violence.[10] In comparison, the NVAW Survey found that only 1.3 percent of surveyed women and 0.9 percent of surveyed men were physically assaulted by a current or former intimate partner annually. The disparity in NFVS and NVAW findings is particularly striking because both surveys used similar behaviorally specific questions to screen respondents for physical assault victimization.

As discussed in this report (see "Deciphering Disparities in Survey Findings"), studies are needed to determine why the NCVS, NFVS, and NVAW Survey produced such disparate findings on the prevalence and incidence of intimate partner violence in the United States.

Intimate partner stalking

Prior to the NVAW Survey, information on stalking prevalence was limited to guesses provided by mental health professionals based on their work with known stalkers. The most frequently cited "guesstimate" was made by forensic psychiatrist Dr. Park Dietz, who reported in 1992 that 5 percent of U.S. women are stalked at some time in their lifetime, and 500,000 are stalked annually.[11] Because these figures pertain to stalking by all types of perpetrators, not just intimates, it is fair to say the NVAW Survey estimates—that 4.8 percent of women have been stalked by an intimate in their lifetime and 503,485 women are stalked by an intimate each year—are higher than previous stalking estimates.

Notes

1. The National Women's Study generated estimates of the prevalence of rape by all types of assailants but not by intimates; see *Rape in America: A Report to the Nation*, Arlington, Virginia: National Victim Center and the Crime Victims Research and Treatment Center, April 23, 1992.

2. Russell, D.E.H., *Rape in Marriage,* Indianapolis: Indiana University Press, 1990.

3. Finklehor, D., and K. Yllo, *License To Rape: Sexual Abuse of Wives,* New York: Holt, Rinehart, and Winston, 1985.

4. Bachman, R., and L.E. Saltzman, *Violence Against Women: Estimates From the Redesigned Survey,* Special Report, Washington, D.C.: U.S. Department of Justice, Bureau of Justice Statistics, 1995, NCJ 154348.

5. Bureau of Justice Statistics, *Bureau of Justice Statistics Sourcebook of Criminal Justice Statistics—1997*, Washington, D.C.: U.S. Department of Justice, Bureau of Justice Statistics, 1998: 198, NCJ 171147, table 3.39.

6. Bachman and Saltzman, *Violence Against Women: Estimates From the Redesigned Survey,* note 4.

7. Greenfeld, L., M.R. Rand, D. Craven, P.A. Klaus, C.A. Perkins, C. Ringel, G. Warchol, C. Matson, and J.A. Fox, *Violence by Intimates: Analysis of Data on Crimes by Current or Former Spouses, Boyfriends, and Girlfriends*, Bureau of Justice Statistics Factbook, Washington, D.C.: U.S. Department of Justice, Bureau of Justice Statistics, 1998, NCJ 167237.

8. Straus, M., and R. Gelles, "Societal Change and Change in Family Violence From 1975 to 1985 as Revealed by Two National Surveys," *Journal of Marriage and the Family* 48 (1987): 465–479.

9. Straus, M.A., "Trends in Cultural Norms and Rates of Partner Violence: An Update to 1992," in *Understanding Partner Violence: Prevalence, Causes, Consequences, and Solutions*, Families in Focus Series, eds. M.A. Straus and S.M. Smith, Minneapolis: National Council on Family Relations, 1995: 30–33.

10. Schafer, J., R. Caetano, and C.L. Clark, "Rates of Intimate Partner Violence in the United States," *American Journal of Public Health* 88 (11) (1998): 1702–1704.

11. Puente, M., "Legislators Tackling the Terror of Stalking: But Some Experts Say Measures Are Vague," *USA Today*, July 21, 1992.

Women Experience More Intimate Partner Violence Than Do Men

As shown in exhibit 1, the NVAW Survey found that women were significantly more likely than men to report being victimized by an intimate partner, whether the period was the individual's lifetime or the 12 months preceding the survey and whether the type of violence was rape, physical assault, or stalking. Moreover, the survey found that differences between women's and men's rates of physical assault by an intimate partner become greater as the seriousness of the assault increases. For example, women were two or three times more likely than men to report that an intimate partner threw something that could hurt them or pushed, grabbed, or shoved them. However, they were 7 to 14 times more likely to report that an intimate partner beat them up, choked or tried to drown them, or threatened them with a gun or knife (exhibit 3).

The NVAW Survey finding that women are significantly more likely than men to report being victimized by an intimate partner supports results from the NCVS, which have consistently shown that women are at significantly greater risk of intimate partner violence (see note 3 in "Introduction"). However, it contradicts results from the NFVS, which have consistently shown that men and women are nearly equally likely to be physically assaulted by marital or cohabiting partners (see note 2 in "Introduction").

Deciphering Disparities in Survey Findings

It is difficult to explain why the NCVS, NFVS, and NVAW Survey generated such disparate estimates of intimate partner violence or why the NCVS and NVAW Survey produced evidence of asymmetry in women's and men's risk of intimate partner violence while the NFVS produced evidence of symmetry. For years, researchers have attributed the low rate of intimate partner violence uncovered by the NCVS to the fact that it is administered in the context of a crime survey. Because they reflect only violence perpetrated by intimates that victims are willing to label as criminal and report to interviewers, estimates of intimate partner violence generated from the NCVS are thought to underestimate the true amount of intimate partner violence.[1]

At first glance, results from the NVAW Survey appear to support this theory. The NVAW Survey—which was administered in the context of a survey on personal safety rather than crime—generated substantially higher intimate partner victimization rates than those generated by the NCVS. It is likely, however, that methodological factors other than the overall context in which the two surveys were administered account for some of the differences in the findings.

For example, the two surveys differ substantially with respect to sample design and survey administration. The NVAW Survey sample was drawn by random-digit dialing from a database of households with a telephone (see sidebar, "Survey Methodology"). Moreover, NVAW Survey interviewers used state-of-the-art techniques to protect the confidentiality of the respondents and minimize the potential for retraumatizing victims of violence. In comparison, the NCVS sample consists of housing units (e.g., addresses) selected from a stratified multistage cluster sample. When a sample unit is

selected for inclusion in the NCVS, U.S. Census workers interview all individuals in the household 12 years of age and older every 6 months for 3 years. Thus, after the first interview, respondents know the contents of the survey. This may pose a problem for victims of domestic violence who may be afraid that disclosing abuse by a family member may put them in danger of further abuse. Although census interviewers document whether others were present during the interview, time and budget constraints prevent them from ensuring privacy during an interview.

In addition, screening questions used by the NVAW Survey and the NCVS differ substantially. For example, the NVAW Survey uses 5 questions to screen respondents for rapes they may have sustained over their lifetime and 12 questions to screen respondents for physical assaults they may have sustained as adults (see sidebar, "Survey Screening Questions"). Respondents disclosing victimization are asked additional questions about the victim-perpetrator relationship and the frequency, duration, and consequences of their victimization. In comparison, the NCVS uses four questions—each with multiple components—to screen respondents for threats, physical and sexual attacks, and property crimes they may have experienced in different locations and by different offenders.[2] Although empirical data on this issue are lacking, researchers assume that both the number of screening questions used and the manner in which they are asked affect disclosure rates.[3]

Another possible reason for the difference in the NVAW Survey and NCVS findings is that published NCVS estimates count series victimization—reports of six or more crimes within a 6-month period for which the respondent cannot recall details of each crime—as a single victimization. Thus, published

Survey Methodology

The National Violence Against Women (NVAW) Survey was conducted from November 1995 to May 1996 by interviewers at Schulman, Ronca, Bucuvalas, Inc. (SRBI) under the direction of John Boyle.[a] The authors of this report designed the survey and conducted the analysis.

The sample was drawn by random-digit dialing from a database of households with a telephone in the 50 States and the District of Columbia. The sample was administered by U.S. Census region. Within each region, a simple random sample of working residential "hundreds banks" of phone numbers was drawn. (A hundreds bank is the first 8 digits of any 10-digit telephone number.) A randomly generated 2-digit number was appended to each randomly sampled hundreds bank to produce the full 10-digit, random-digit number. Separate banks of numbers were generated for male and female respondents. These random-digit numbers were called by SRBI interviewers from their central telephone facility, where nonworking and nonresidential numbers were screened out. Once a residential household was reached, eligible adults were identified. In households with more than one eligible adult, the adult with the most recent birthday was selected as the designated respondent.

A total of 8,000 women and 8,005 men 18 years of age and older were interviewed using a computer-assisted telephone interviewing (CATI) system. (Five completed interviews with men were subsequently eliminated from the sample during data editing due to an excessive amount of inconsistent and missing data.) Only female interviewers surveyed female respondents. To test for possible bias introduced by the gender of the interviewer, a split-sample approach was used in the male sample whereby half of the interviews were conducted by female interviewers and half by male interviewers. A Spanish-language translation was administered by bilingual interviewers to Spanish-speaking respondents.

To determine how representative the sample was, select demographic characteristics of the NVAW Survey sample were compared with demographic characteristics of the general population as measured by the U.S. Census Bureau's 1995 Current Population Survey of adult men and women. Sample weighting was considered to correct for possible biases introduced by the fact that some households had multiple phone lines and multiple eligibles and for over- and underrepresentation of selected subgroups. Although there were some instances of over- and underrepresentation, the overall unweighted prevalence rates for rape, physical assault, and stalking were not significantly different from their respective weighted rates. As a result, sample weighting was not used in the analysis of the survey data.[b]

Data were analyzed using SPSS Base 7.0 for Windows software. Measures of association were calculated between nominal-level independent and dependent variables. The chi-square statistic was used to test for statistically significant differences between two groups (e.g., men and women), and the Tukey's B statistic was used to test for statistically significant differences among two or more groups (e.g., whites, African-Americans, Asian/Pacific Islanders, American Indian/Alaska Natives, and mixed-race persons). Any estimates based on fewer than five responses were deemed unreliable and, therefore, were not tested for statistically significant differences between or among groups and were not presented in the tables. Because estimates presented in this report generally exclude "don't know," "refused," and other invalid responses, sample and subsample sizes (*n*'s) vary from table to table.

Because the actual number of victims that is insufficient to reliably calculate estimates varies depending on the rarity of the exposure and the denominator of the subgroup being analyzed, the relative standard error (RSE) was calculated for each estimate presented. (RSE is the ratio of the standard error divided by the actual point estimate.) Estimates with RSEs that exceed 30 percent were deemed unstable and were not tested for statistically significant differences between or among groups. These estimates have been identified in the tables and should be viewed with caution.

The estimates from this survey, as from any sample survey, are subject to random sampling error. Exhibit 4 presents the estimated standard errors multiplied by the *z*-score (1.96) for specified sample and subsample sizes of 16,000 or less at different response distributions of dichotomous variables (e.g., raped/not raped, injured/not injured). These estimated standard errors can be used to determine the extent to which sample estimates will be distributed (bounded) around the population parameter (i.e., the true population distribution). As exhibit 4 shows, larger sample and subsample sizes produce smaller estimated bounds. Thus, the estimated bound at the 95-percent confidence level for a sample or subsample of 8,000 is 1.1 percentage points if the response distribution is a 50/50 split, whereas the estimated bound at the 95-percent confidence level for a sample or subsample of 50 is 14 percentage points if the response distribution is a 50/50 split.

---

a. John Boyle, Ph.D., is senior vice president and director of the Government and Social Research Division at SRBI. Dr. Boyle, who specializes in public policy research in the area of health and violence, also manages the firm's Washington, D.C., office.

b. A technical report describing the survey methods in more detail and recording sample characteristics and prevalence rates using weighted and unweighted data will be available from the Centers for Disease Control and Prevention (see sidebar, "Other Publications in the Series").

NCVS estimates of the number of intimate partner rapes, sexual assaults, and physical assaults are lower than would be obtained by including all incidents reported to its survey interviewers. To produce NCVS estimates more directly comparable to those generated by the NVAW Survey, each crime in a series of victimizations reported to NCVS interviewers would have to be counted.

Finally, the sampling errors associated with the estimates from the NVAW Survey and the NCVS would have to be compared to determine whether estimates generated by the two surveys actually differ or whether apparent differences are not statistically significant.

Differences between the NVAW Survey and the NFVS estimates are somewhat harder to explain because the two surveys used similar sampling strategies and the Conflict Tactics Scale to screen respondents for physical assaults by intimates (see sidebar, "Survey Screening Questions"). Straus argues the NVAW Survey generated annual rates of physical assault by an intimate partner that were substantially lower than those generated by the NFVS because it was presented to respondents as a survey on personal safety.[4] According to Straus, the term "personal safety" led many respondents to perceive the NVAW Survey as a crime study and, therefore, to restrict their reports to "real crimes."

Size of Sample or Subsample	Exhibit 4. Estimated Standard Errors Multiplied by the *z*-Score (1.96) for a 95-Percent Confidence Level, by Sample or Subsample Size				
	Percentage of Sample or Subsample Giving Certain Response or Displaying Certain Characteristics for Percentages Exactly or Approximately Equal to:				
	10 or 90	**20 or 80**	**30 or 70**	**40 or 60**	**50**
16,000	0.5	0.6	0.7	0.8	0.8
12,000	0.6	0.7	0.8	0.9	0.9
8,000	0.7	0.9	1.0	1.1	1.1
4,000	0.9	1.2	1.4	1.5	1.5
3,000	1.1	1.4	1.6	1.8	1.8
2,000	1.3	1.8	2.0	2.1	2.2
1,500	1.5	2.0	2.3	2.5	2.5
1,300	1.6	2.2	2.5	2.7	2.7
1,200	1.7	2.3	2.6	2.8	2.8
1,100	1.8	2.4	2.7	2.9	3.0
1,000	1.9	2.5	2.8	3.0	3.1
900	2.0	2.6	3.0	3.2	3.3
800	2.1	2.8	3.2	3.4	3.5
700	2.2	3.0	3.4	3.6	3.7
600	2.4	3.2	3.7	3.9	4.0
500	2.6	3.5	4.0	4.3	4.4
400	2.9	3.9	4.5	4.8	4.9
300	3.4	4.5	5.2	5.6	5.7
200	4.2	5.6	6.4	6.8	6.9
150	4.8	6.4	7.4	7.9	8.0
100	5.9	7.9	9.0	9.7	9.8
75	6.8	9.1	10.4	11.2	11.4
50	8.4	11.2	12.8	13.7	14.0

Aside from being inherently unconvincing—the terms "crime" and "personal safety" conjure very different images—this explanation fails to explain why the NVAW Survey generated high lifetime intimate partner victimization rates that are generally consistent with findings from other surveys or why the NVAW Survey uncovered high rates of other forms of family violence, such as incest and physical abuse of children by adult caretakers.[5] It is unlikely that using the term "personal safety" in the NVAW Survey introduction would have set up a perceptual screen for intimate partner violence experienced in the previous 12 months but not for intimate partner violence experienced over the course of the respondent's lifetime. Similarly, it is unlikely that using the term "personal safety" in the NVAW Survey introduction would have set up a perceptual screen for one type of family violence (e.g., physical assaults

by marital/cohabiting partners) but not for other types of family violence (e.g., incest and physical assault by caretakers in childhood).

A more plausible explanation for the disparity in the NFVS and NVAW Survey findings is the different ways the two surveys frame and introduce screening questions about intimate partner violence. In the NFVS, respondents are queried about specific acts of intimate partner violence they may have committed or sustained against their current partner. Published NFVS estimates of the number of women and men who experience intimate partner violence annually count reports of both perpetration and victimization. In other words, if a woman reports that she assaulted her husband, her report is counted as a male victimization. Similarly, if a man reports that he assaulted his wife, his report is counted as a female victimization. To produce NFVS estimates directly comparable with NVAW Survey estimates, perpetrations reported to NFVS interviewers would have to be excluded.

In addition, the NFVS introduces screening questions about intimate partner violence perpetration and victimization with an exculpatory statement that acknowledges the pervasiveness of marital/partner conflict. Although this approach may seem more accepting of intimate partner violence and, therefore, more likely to result in disclosure of intimate partner violence, it may also be considered more leading.

Finally, the NFVS frames its screening questions in terms of how many times in the past 12 months respondents have committed or sustained these violent acts rather than whether they have ever committed or sustained these violent acts. This approach assumes intimate partner violence is the norm and requires respondents who neither committed nor sustained such violence to provide an answer to the contrary.

By contrast, the NVAW Survey queries respondents only about their experiences with victimization. Furthermore, the NVAW Survey does not use an exculpatory statement to introduce screening questions. Rather than asking respondents how many times they have sustained acts of intimate partner violence in the past 12 months, the NVAW Survey asks respondents whether they ever sustained violent acts at the hands of any type of perpetrator and, if so, whether their perpetrator was a current or past intimate partner. Only respondents who report they have ever experienced such acts are asked whether these acts were perpetrated in the past 12 months. While this approach may be considered less accepting of intimate partner violence and therefore less likely to result in disclosure, it may also be considered less leading.

In summary, it is likely that the manner in which screening questions are introduced and framed has more of an effect on intimate partner victimization rates than does the overall context in which the survey is administered. Clearly, more research is needed to fully understand how methodological factors such as sample design, survey administration, survey introduction, and question wording affect research findings on intimate partner violence.

Notes

1. Klaus, P., and M. Rand, *Family Violence*, Special Report, Washington, D.C.: U.S. Department of Justice, Bureau of Justice Statistics, 1984, NCJ 093449; Straus, M.A., "Physical Assault by Wives: A Major Social Problem," in *Current Controversies on Family Violence*, eds. R.J. Gelles and D.R. Loeske, Newbury Park, California: Sage Publications, 1993: 67–87.

2. The four screening questions used in the NCVS are:

1) *Were you attacked or threatened, OR did you have something stolen from you:*

   a) *At home, including the porch or yard?*
   b) *At or near a friend's, relative's, or neighbor's home?*
   c) *At work or school?*
   d) *In a place such as a storage shed or laundry room, a shopping mall, restaurant, bank, or airport?*
   e) *While riding in any vehicle?*
   f) *On the street or in a parking lot?*
   g) *At such places as a party, theater, gym, picnic area, bowling lanes, or while fishing or hunting?*

2) *Other than any incidents already mentioned, has anyone attacked or threatened you in any of these ways:*

   a) *With any weapon, for instance, a gun or knife?*
   b) *With anything like a baseball bat, frying pan, scissors, or a stick?*
   c) *By something thrown, such as a rock or bottle?*
   d) *Include any grabbing, punching, or choking?*
   e) *Any rape, attempted rape, or other type of sexual attack?*

f) Any face-to-face threats?
g) Any attack or threat of use of force by
anyone at all?

Please mention it even if you are not certain
it was a crime.

3) *People often don't think of incidents committed*
by someone they know. Did you have some
thing stolen from you, OR were you attacked or
threatened by:

a) Someone at work or school?
b) A neighbor or friend?
c) A relative or family member?
d) Any other person you've met or known?

4) *Incidents involving forced or unwanted*
sexual acts are often difficult to talk about.
Have you been forced or coerced to engage
in unwanted sexual activity by:

a) Someone you didn't know before?
b) A casual acquaintance?
c) Someone you know well?

3. For example, see Helton, A.M., "The Pregnant Battered Women," *Responses to Victimization of Women and Children* 9 (1) (1986): 22–23; Koss, M.P., "Detecting the Scope of Rape: A Review of Prevalence Research Methods," *Journal of Interpersonal Violence* 8 (2) (1993): 198–222; Schuman, H., and S. Presser, *Questions and Answers in Attitude Surveys: Experiments on Question Form, Wording, and Content*, New York: Academic Press, Inc., 1981; Sudman, S., and N.M. Bradburn, *Response Effects in Surveys: A Review and Synthesis*, Chicago: Aldine Publishing Company, 1974.

4. Straus, M.A., "The Controversy Over Domestic Violence by Women: A Methodological, Theoretical, and Sociology of Science Analysis," in *Violence in Intimate Relationships,* eds. X.B. Arriaga and S. Oskamp, Thousand Oaks, California: Sage Publications, 1999.

5. For example, 40 percent of surveyed women and 54 percent of surveyed men said they were physically assaulted as a child by an adult caretaker. In addition, 9 percent of surveyed women said they were raped before age 18. Of these rape victims, 76 percent were raped by a relative. See Tjaden, P., and N. Thoennes, *Final Report on Prevalence, Incidence, and Consequences of Violence Against Women,* Washington, D.C.: U.S. Department of Justice, National Institute of Justice, forthcoming.

Prevalence of Intimate Partner Violence Among Racial Minorities and Hispanics

As noted, previous studies have produced contradictory findings as to whether race and ethnicity affect one's risk for involvement in intimate partner violence (see notes 4 and 5 in "Introduction"). Most of these studies compare victimization rates of only one minority group with those of whites, and others compare victimization rates of all minority groups with those of whites. None compare victimization rates of several diverse racial groups.

To determine victimization rates for women and men of diverse racial backgrounds, respondents to the NVAW Survey were asked whether they would best classify themselves as white, black or African-American, Asian or Pacific Islander, American Indian or Alaska Native, or of mixed race. They were also asked whether they were of Hispanic origin. The response rate on both these questions was very high (98 and 99 percent, respectively).

When data on African-American, Asian/Pacific Islander, American Indian/Alaska Native, and mixed-race respondents are combined, nonwhite women and men report significantly more intimate partner violence than do their white counterparts (exhibit 5). These findings suggest that all racial minorities experience more intimate partner violence than do whites.

However, a comparison of intimate partner victimization rates among persons of specific racial backgrounds shows that different types of minorities report significantly different rates of intimate partner violence. In general, American Indian/ Alaska Native women report significantly higher rates of intimate partner violence than do women of other racial backgrounds, and Asian/Pacific Islander women and men report significantly lower rates (exhibit 6). These findings underscore the need for research on intimate partner violence among specific racial and ethnic groups. As the

Exhibit 5. Persons Victimized by an Intimate Partner in Lifetime, by Victim Gender, Type of Victimization, and White/Nonwhite Status of Victim		
	Persons Victimized in Lifetime (%)	
Victim Gender/Type of Victimization	White	Nonwhite[a]
Women	(n = 6,452)	(n = 1,398)
Rape	7.7	7.8
Physical assault[b***]	21.3	25.5
Stalking	4.7	5.0
Total victimized[b**]	24.8	28.6
Men	(n = 6,424)	(n = 1,335)
Rape	0.2	0.5[c]
Physical assault[b**]	7.2	9.1
Stalking[b*]	0.6	1.1
Total victimized[b**]	7.5	10.0

[a]The nonwhite category consists of African-American, Native American/Alaska Native, Asian/Pacific Islander, and mixed-race respondents.

[b]Differences between whites and nonwhites are statistically significant: χ^2, $*p \leq .05$, $**p \leq .01$, $***p \leq .001$.

[c]Relative standard error exceeds 30 percent; statistical tests not performed.

Exhibit 6. Persons Victimized by an Intimate Partner in Lifetime, by Victim Gender, Type of Victimization, and Victim Race					
Victim Gender/ Type of Victimization	**Persons Victimized in Lifetime (%)**				
	White	**African- American**	**Asian Pacific Islander**	**American Indian/ Alaska Native**	**Mixed Race**
Women	(n = 6,452)	(n = 780)	(n = 133)	(n = 88)	(n = 397)
Rape[a]	7.7	7.4	3.8[b]	15.9	8.1
Physical assault[c,d]	21.3	26.3	12.8	30.7	27.0
Stalking	4.7	4.2	—[e]	10.2[b]	6.3
Total victimized[c]	24.8	29.1	15.0	37.5	30.2
Men	(n = 6,424)	(n = 659)	(n = 165)	(n = 105)	(n = 406)
Rape	0.2	0.9[b]	—[e]	—[e]	—[e]
Physical assault	7.2	10.8	—[e]	11.4	8.6
Stalking	0.6	1.1[b]	—[e]	—[e]	1.2[b]
Total victimized	7.5	12.0	3.0[b]	12.4	9.1

[a]Estimates for American Indian/Alaska Native women are significantly higher than those for white and African-American women: Tukey's B, $p \le .05$.

[b]Relative standard error exceeds 30 percent; estimates not included in statistical testing.

[c]Estimates for Asian/Pacific Islander women are significantly lower than those for African-American, American Indian/Alaska Native, and mixed-race women: Tukey's B, $p \le .05$.

[d]Estimates for African-American women are significantly higher than those for white women: Tukey's B, $p \le .05$.

[e]Estimates not calculated on fewer than five victims.

survey results show, combining data on different minorities may exaggerate differences between whites and nonwhites and, at the same time, obscure very large differences among persons of diverse minority backgrounds.

The finding that American Indians/Alaska Native women report significantly higher rates of intimate partner violence is consistent with previous research that shows American Indian couples are significantly more violent than their white counterparts.[1] However, a paucity of information on violence against American Indians makes it difficult to explain why they report more intimate partner violence. How much of the difference in intimate partner victimization rates among American Indian/Alaska Native women and those of other racial backgrounds may be explained by differences in willingness to report victimization to interviewers and how much by actual victimization experiences is unclear and requires further study. Moreover, there

may be significant differences in intimate partner victimization rates among women (and men) of diverse American Indian tribes and Alaska Native communities that cannot be discerned from the survey. Finally, research is needed to ascertain how much of the difference in intimate partner victimization rates among Native Americans and persons of different racial backgrounds may be explained by demographic, social, and environmental factors.

Because information on violence against Asian/Pacific Islander women and men is also limited, it is difficult to explain why they reported significantly less intimate partner violence than did women and men of other racial backgrounds. It has been suggested that traditional Asian values emphasizing close family ties and harmony may discourage Asian women from disclosing physical and emotional abuse by intimates.[2] Thus, the lower intimate partner victimization rates found among Asian/Pacific Islander women may be, at least in part, an artifact of underreporting. There may also be significant differences in rates of intimate partner violence between Asian and Pacific Islander women that cannot be discerned from the survey because data on these two groups are combined. Finally, there may be significant differences between Asian/Pacific Islander women born in this country and those who immigrated. A recent nonrepresentative study of immigrant Korean women found that 60 percent had been battered by their husbands.[3] Clearly, more research is recommended on violence committed by intimates against Asian and Pacific Islander women.

The survey found little difference in Hispanic and non-Hispanic women's reports of intimate partner physical assault and intimate partner stalking. However, Hispanic women were significantly more likely than non-Hispanic women to report that they were raped by a current or former intimate partner at some time in their lifetime (exhibit 7). These findings are noteworthy because previously published NVAW Survey findings show that Hispanic women report sig-

nificantly less rape victimization than do non-Hispanic women when all types of perpetrators are considered.[4] Future research should focus on why Hispanic women are less likely to be raped by a nonintimate but more likely to be raped by an intimate.

The survey found no significant difference in reports of intimate partner violence among Hispanic and non-Hispanic men (exhibit 7). However, this finding must be viewed with caution, given the small number of Hispanic male victims.

Notes

1. Bachman, R., *Death and Violence on the Reservation: Homicide, Family Violence, and Suicide in American Indian Populations*, Westport, Connecticut: Auburn House, 1992.

2. National Research Council, *Understanding Violence Against Women,* Washington, D.C.: National Academy Press, 1996: 40–41.

Exhibit 7. Persons Victimized by an Intimate Partner in Lifetime, by Victim Gender, Type of Victimization, and Hispanic/Non-Hispanic Origin of Victim		
Victim Gender/Type of Victimization	**Persons Victimized in Lifetime (%)**	
	Hispanic[a]	Non-Hispanic
Women	(*n* = 628)	(*n* = 7,317)
Rape[b]	7.9	5.7
Physical assault	21.2	22.1
Stalking	4.8	4.8
Total victimized	23.4	25.6
Men	(*n* = 581)	(*n* = 7,335)
Rape	—[c]	0.3
Physical assault	6.5	7.5
Stalking	—[c]	0.7
Total victimized	7.4	8.0

[a]Persons of Hispanic origin may be of any race.
[b]Differences between Hispanics and non-Hispanics are statistically significant: χ^2, $p \leq .05$.
[c]Estimates not calculated on fewer than five victims.

3. Song, Y.I., "Battered Korean Women in Urban America: The Relationship of Cultural Conflict to Wife Abuse," unpublished doctoral dissertation, Ohio State University, Columbus, 1986.

4. Tjaden, P., and N. Thoennes, *Prevalence, Incidence, and Consequences of Violence Against Women: Findings From the National Violence Against Women Survey,* Research in Brief; Washington, D.C.: U.S. Department of Justice, National Institute of Justice, 1998, NCJ 172837.

Prevalence of Intimate Partner Violence Among Same-Sex Cohabitants

Research on violence in same-sex relationships has been limited to studies of small, unrepresentative samples of gay and lesbian couples. Results from these studies suggest that same-sex couples are about as violent as heterosexual couples.[1]

Although the NVAW Survey did not ask respondents about their sexual orientation, it did ask them whether they had ever lived with a same-sex partner as part of a couple. As such, it is possible to compare intimate partner victimization rates among women and men who have a history of same-sex cohabitation with women and men who have a history of marital/opposite-sex cohabitation only.

The survey found that 1 percent of surveyed women ($n = 79$) and 0.8 percent of surveyed men ($n = 65$) reported living with a same-sex intimate partner at least once in their lifetime, and 90 percent of surveyed women ($n = 7,193$) and 86 percent of surveyed men ($n = 6,879$) reported marrying/ living with an opposite-sex partner but never with a same-sex partner. For brevity's sake, the former will be referred to as same-sex cohabitants and the latter will be referred to as opposite-sex cohabitants. It is unknown how many same-sex or opposite-sex cohabitants identified themselves as homosexual, bisexual, or heterosexual at the time of the interview.

Exhibit 8. Persons Victimized by an Intimate Partner in Lifetime, by Victim Gender, Type of Victimization, and History of Same-Sex/Opposite-Sex Cohabitation

Victim Gender/Type of Victimization	Persons Victimized in Lifetime (%)	
	History of Same-Sex Cohabitation[a]	History of Opposite-Sex Cohabitation[b]
Women	($n = 79$)	($n = 7,193$)
Rape	11.4[c]	4.4
Physical assault[d*]	35.4	20.4
Stalking	—[e]	4.1
Total victimized[d**]	39.2	21.7
Men	($n = 65$)	($n = 6,879$)
Rape	—[e]	0.2
Physical assault[d*]	21.5	7.1
Stalking	—[e]	0.5
Total victimized[d**]	23.1	7.4

[a]Subsample consists of respondents who have ever lived with a same-sex intimate partner.
[b]Subsample consists of respondents who have ever married and/or lived with an opposite-sex intimate partner but never with a same-sex intimate partner.
[c]Relative standard error exceeds 30 percent; statistical tests not performed.
[d]Differences between same-sex and opposite-sex cohabitants are statistically significant: χ^2, *$p \leq .01$, **$p \leq .001$.
[e]Estimates not calculated on fewer than five individuals.

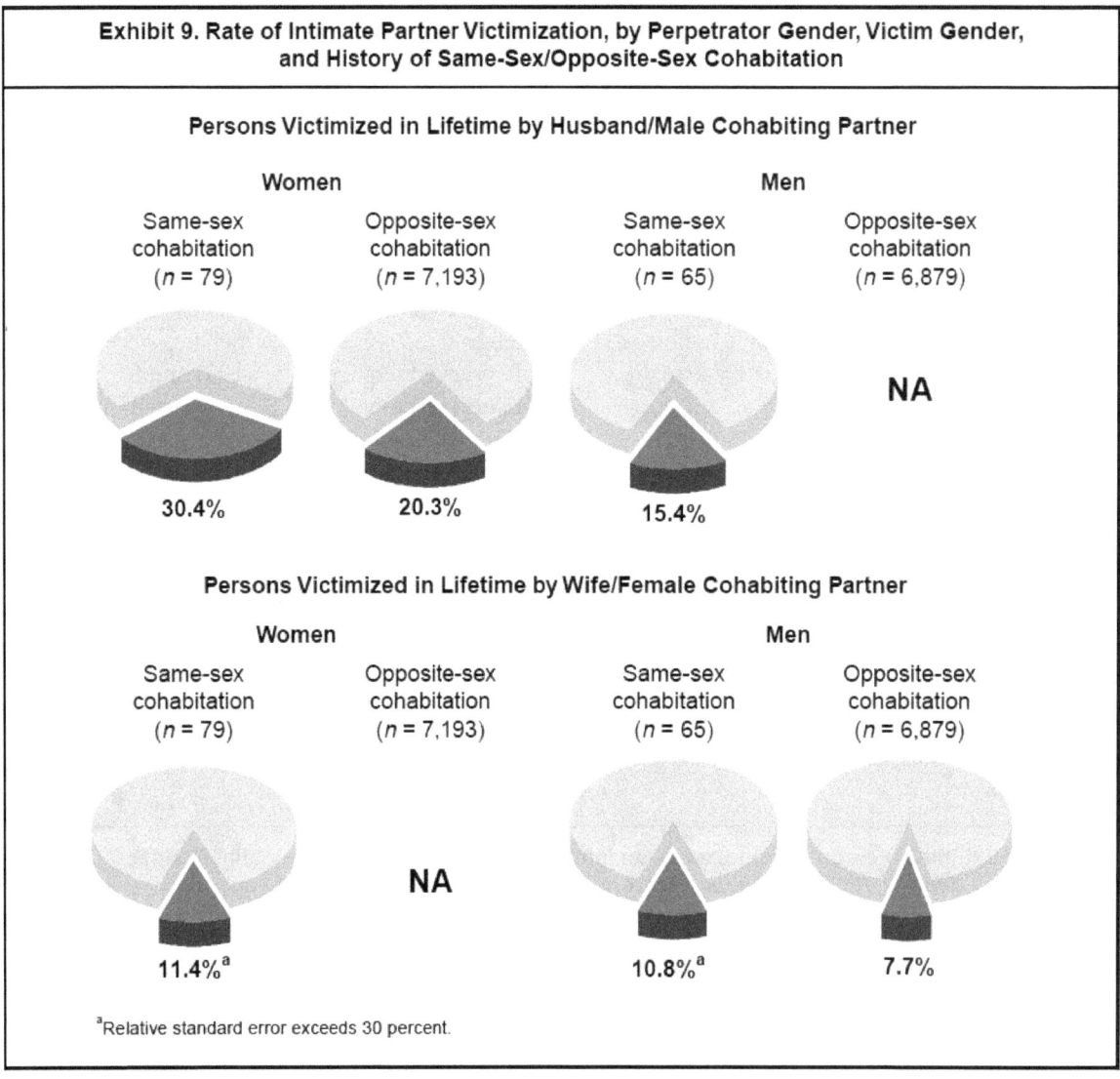

Exhibit 9. Rate of Intimate Partner Victimization, by Perpetrator Gender, Victim Gender, and History of Same-Sex/Opposite-Sex Cohabitation

Persons Victimized in Lifetime by Husband/Male Cohabiting Partner

Women

Same-sex cohabitation (*n* = 79) — 30.4%

Opposite-sex cohabitation (*n* = 7,193) — 20.3%

Men

Same-sex cohabitation (*n* = 65) — 15.4%

Opposite-sex cohabitation (*n* = 6,879) — NA

Persons Victimized in Lifetime by Wife/Female Cohabiting Partner

Women

Same-sex cohabitation (*n* = 79) — 11.4%[a]

Opposite-sex cohabitation (*n* = 7,193) — NA

Men

Same-sex cohabitation (*n* = 65) — 10.8%[a]

Opposite-sex cohabitation (*n* = 6,879) — 7.7%

[a]Relative standard error exceeds 30 percent.

The survey found that same-sex cohabitants reported significantly more intimate partner violence than did opposite-sex cohabitants. Among women, 39.2 percent of the same-sex cohabitants and 21.7 percent of the opposite-sex cohabitants reported being raped, physically assaulted, and/or stalked by a marital/cohabiting partner at some time in their lifetime. Among men, the comparable figures are 23.1 percent and 7.4 percent (exhibit 8).

At first glance, these findings suggest that both male and female same-sex couples experience more intimate partner violence than do opposite-sex couples. However, a comparison of intimate partner victimization rates among same-sex and opposite-sex cohabitants by perpetrator gender produced some interesting findings: 30.4 percent of same-sex cohabiting women reported being victimized by a male partner, whereas 11.4 percent reported being victimized by a female partner. Thus, same-sex cohabiting women were nearly three times more likely to report being victimized by a male partner than by a female partner. Moreover, opposite-sex cohabiting women were nearly twice as likely to report being victimized by a male partner than were same-sex cohabiting women by a female partner (20.3 percent and 11.4 percent) (exhibit 9).

Somewhat different patterns were found for men. Like their female counterparts, same-sex cohabiting men were more likely to report being victimized by a male partner than by a female partner. Specifically, 15.4 percent of same-sex cohabiting men reported being raped, physically assaulted, and/or stalked by a male partner, but 10.8 percent reported such violence by a female partner. However, same-sex cohabiting men were nearly twice as likely to report being victimized by a male partner than were opposite-sex cohabiting men by a female partner (15.4 percent and 7.7 percent). These findings suggest that intimate partner violence is perpetrated primarily by men, whether against male or female partners.

Note

1. Brand, P., and A. Kidd, "Frequency of Physical Aggression in Heterosexual and Female Homosexual Dyads," *Psychological Reports* 59 (1986): 1307–1313; Lie, G., and S. Gentlewarrior, "Intimate Violence in Lesbian Relationships: Discussion of Survey Findings and Practice Implications," *Journal of Social Service Research* 15 (1991): 41–59; Lockhart, L., B. White, V. Causby, and A. Issac, "Letting Out the Secret: Violence in Lesbian Relationships," *Journal of Interpersonal Violence* 9 (1994): 469–492; Perry, S., "Lesbian Alcohol and Marijuana Use: Correlates of HIV Risk Behaviors and Abusive Relationships," *Journal of Proactive Drugs* 27 (1995): 413–419; Renzetti, C.M., "Violence and Abuse Among Same-Sex Couples," in *Violence Between Intimate Partners: Patterns, Causes, and Effects*, ed. A.P. Cardarelli, Boston: Allyn and Bacon, 1997: 70–89; Schilit, R., G. Lie, and M. Montagne, "Substance Use as a Correlate of Violence in Intimate Lesbian Relationships," *Journal of Homosexuality* 19 (1990): 51–65; Waldner-Haugrud, L.K., L.V. Gratch, and B. Magruder, "Victimization and Perpetration Rates of Violence in Gay and Lesbian Relationships: Gender Issues Explored," *Violence and Victims* 12 (2) (1997): 173–184; Waldner-Haugrud, L.K., and L.V. Gratch, "Sexual Coercion in Gay/Lesbian Relationships: Descriptives and Gender Differences," *Violence and Victims* 12 (1) (1997): 87–98; Waterman, C., L. Dawson, and M. Bologna, "Sexual Coercion in Gay Male and Lesbian Relationships: Predictors and Implications for Support Services," *Journal of Sex Research* 26 (1989): 118–124.

Risk Factors Associated With Intimate Partner Violence

Risk factors are characteristics associated with an increased likelihood that a problem behavior will occur. It is important to note that the presence of a risk factor does not mean that the behavior will necessarily occur, only that the odds of it occurring are greater.

Numerous studies have examined risk factors associated with intimate partner violence. Results from these studies show that unmarried, cohabiting couples have higher rates of intimate partner violence than do married couples[1]; minorities have higher rates of intimate partner violence than do whites (see note 5 in "Introduction"); lower income women have higher rates of intimate partner violence than do higher income women[2]; less educated women have higher rates of intimate partner violence than do more educated women[3]; and couples with income, educational, or occupational status disparities have higher rates of intimate partner violence than do couples with no status disparity.[4] Research also shows that experiencing and/or witnessing violence in one's family of origin increases one's chances of being a perpetrator or victim of intimate partner violence.[5] In addition, research shows that wife assault is more common in families where power is concentrated in the hands of the husband or male partner and the husband makes most of the decisions regarding family finances and strictly controls when and where his wife or female partner goes.[6] Finally, research suggests that persons with a disability are at greater risk of violence,[7] although there is no empirical evidence that having a disability increases one's risk of intimate partner violence.

To increase understanding of risk factors associated with intimate partner violence, logistic regressions were conducted using a backward stepwise procedure on respondents married or cohabiting with a partner at the time of the interview to determine what characteristics of the relationship, respondent, or partner differentiated those who reported being victimized by their current partner from those who did not. Separate analyses were conducted for women ($n = 4,896$) and men ($n = 5,056$).

In each of the logistic regressions, the dependent variable was whether the respondent reported being raped, physically assaulted, or stalked by his or her current spouse or cohabiting partner. The independent variables were as follows:

- Whether the respondent was cohabiting versus married.

- Whether the respondent was white, African-American, American Indian/Alaska Native, Asian/Pacific Islander, or mixed race.

- Whether the respondent was Hispanic.

- Whether the respondent's race and/or Hispanic origin was different from the partner's.

- Whether the respondent's education level was a high school diploma or less.

- Whether the respondent's education level was higher than the partner's.

- Whether the respondent was physically assaulted as a child by an adult caretaker.

- Whether the partner was jealous or possessive.

- Whether the partner denied the respondent access to family, friends, or family income.

- Whether the partner called the respondent names or shouted or swore at the respondent in front of other people.

- Whether the respondent was physically disabled when the relationship started.

The logistic regressions were designed to provide a measure by which the relative importance of the independent variables could be assessed and to determine which variables increased the odds that a woman or man would be victimized by an intimate partner. Income variables were not included in the analyses because of the large number of respondents who refused to provide information about their or their partner's income.

The results of the logistic regression reveal a strong link between child maltreatment and subsequent victimization by an intimate partner. Women and men who were physically assaulted as children by adult caretakers were significantly more likely to report being victimized by their current partner, even when the effects of other independent variables were controlled (see tables I and II in sidebar, "Results of the Logistic Regressions"). It is possible that persons victimized as children by adult caretakers were more tolerant of persons who engaged in violent and threatening behaviors as adults and, therefore, more likely to get involved with abusive partners. However, it is also possible that respondents who reported one type of victimization (e.g., child maltreatment) were simply more willing to report other types of victimization (c.g., intimate partner violence). Clearly, more research is recommended on the possible link between childhood victimization and intimate partner victimization.

Results of the logistic regression for women, but not men, support previous research that shows unmarried couples are at greater risk of intimate partner violence than married couples, and African-American couples are at greater risk than white couples. They also show a strong link between violence and emotionally abusive and controlling behavior in intimate relationships. Indeed, having a verbally abusive partner was associated with the largest change in the odds that a woman would be victimized by an intimate partner (see table I in sidebar, "Results of the Logistic Regressions"). These findings support the theory that much of the

violence perpetrated against women by male partners is part of a systematic pattern of dominance and control, or what some researchers have called "patriarchal terrorism."[8]

Results of the logistic regressions for both women and men support the theory that couples with status disparities experience more intimate partner violence than do couples with no status disparities. Women were significantly more likely to report violence by a current partner if their education level was greater than their partner's, and men were significantly more likely to report being victimized by their current partner if their race and/or Hispanic origin was different from their partner's (see tables I and II in sidebar, "Results of the Logistic Regressions").

Notes

1. Yllo, K., and M. Straus, "Interpersonal Violence Among Married and Cohabiting Couples," *Family Relations* 30 (1981): 339–347; Stets, J.E., and M.A. Straus, "The Marriage License as a Hitting License: A Comparison of Assaults in Dating, Cohabiting, and Married Couples," *Journal of Family Violence* 4 (2) (1989): 161–180; Ellis, L., *Theories of Rape: Inquiries Into the Causes of Sexual Aggression,* New York: Hemisphere Books, 1989.

2. Bachman, R., *Violence Against Women: A National Crime Victimization Survey Report,* Washington, D.C.: U.S. Department of Justice, Bureau of Justice Statistics, 1994, NCJ 145325; Bachman, R., and L.E. Saltzman, *Violence Against Women: Estimates From the Redesigned Survey,* Special Report, Washington, D.C.: U.S. Department of Justice, Bureau of Justice Statistics, 1995, NCJ 154348; *Behind Closed Doors,* eds. Straus, M.A., R.J. Gelles, and S. Steinmetz, Newbury Park, California: Sage Publications, 1980; Zawit, M.W., *Violence Between Intimates,* Washington, D.C.: U.S. Department of Justice, Bureau of Justice Statistics, 1994, NCJ 149259.

3. *Ibid.,* Bachman and Saltzman; *ibid.,* Zawit; Hornung, C.A., B.C. McCullough, and T. Sugimoto, "Status Relationships in Marriage, Risk Factors in Spouse Abuse," *Journal of Marriage and the Family* 43 (1981): 675–692.

Results of the Logistic Regressions

I. **Best Model of the Relationship Between Independent Variables and Risk of Intimate Partner Violence for Women**

Variable	B	S.E.	Exp(b)	p-value
Respondent was cohabiting	0.5562	0.24	1.7441	0.018
Respondent was white	−0.4171	0.17	0.6590	0.021
Respondent was African-American	0.2988	0.24	1.3483	0.014
Respondent was Asian/Pacific Islander	−0.2048	0.40	0.8148	0.208
Respondent was American Indian/Alaska Native	0.3854	0.43	1.4702	0.609
Respondent's education level was higher than partner's	0.3400	0.14	1.4049	0.019
Respondent was physically assaulted as a child by a caretaker	0.9546	0.14	2.5976	0.000
Partner was jealous or possessive	0.9597	0.16	2.6109	0.000
Partner was denied access to family, friends, or income	0.4466	0.21	1.5630	0.031
Partner was verbally abusive	2.0324	0.15	7.6325	0.000
Constant	−4.4202	0.30		

II. **Best Model of the Relationship Between Independent Variables and Risk of Intimate Partner Violence for Men**

Variable	B	S.E.	Exp(b)	p-value
Respondent was cohabiting	−0.4307	0.25	0.6501	0.085
Respondent's race/Hispanic origin was different from partner's	0.6697	0.22	1.9537	0.002
Respondent was physically assaulted as a child by a caretaker	1.1356	0.21	3.1131	0.000
Constant	−4.0239	0.29		

III. **Best Model of the Relationship Between Independent Variables and Risk of Injury for Female Intimate Partner Rape Victims***

Variable	B	S.E.	Exp(b)	p-value
Victim was Hispanic	1.4219	0.66	4.1449	0.031
Victim was 18–25 years old	0.7486	0.41	2.1140	0.070
Perpetrator threatened to harm or kill	1.2620	0.26	3.5324	0.000
Perpetrator used a weapon	0.9467	0.50	2.5773	0.057
Perpetrator was using drugs or alcohol	0.4395	0.27	1.5519	0.010
Perpetrator was a spouse	0.5286	0.26	1.6966	0.041
Perpetrator was a cohabiting partner	−0.7862	0.20	0.4556	0.000
Constant	−1.3332	0.26		

(continued)

36

(continued)				
IV. Best Model of the Relationship Between Independent Variables and Risk of Injury for Female Victims of Intimate Partner Physical Assault*				
Variable	**B**	**S.E.**	**Exp(b)**	**p-value**
Perpetrator threatened to harm or kill	0.9683	0.13	2.6335	0.000
Perpetrator was using drugs or alcohol	0.5225	0.12	1.6863	0.000
Constant	−9.749	0.10		
V. Best Model of the Relationship Between Independent Variables and Risk of Injury for Male Victims of Intimate Partner Physical Assault*				
Variable	**B**	**S.E.**	**Exp(b)**	**p-value**
Perpetrator threatened to harm or kill	0.7987	0.28	2.2226	0.005
Perpetrator used a weapon	0.6341	0.31	1.8865	0.0438
Constant	−1.7944	0.15		

Note: Several statistics are presented in tables I–V. The logistic coefficients (B) and their standard errors (S.E.) can be interpreted as the change associated with a unit change in the explanatory variable when all other variables in the model are held constant. The regression coefficients can be more easily understood if quoted as an odds ratio. The odds ratio [Exp(b)] provides the ratio of the odds of the p (the probability of an event happening) in the group responding *yes* to the explanatory variable relative to the group responding *no* to the explanatory variable while all other variables are held constant. For example, an odds ratio of 1 indicates changes in the explanatory variable do not lead to changes in the odds of p; a ratio of less than 1 indicates the odds of p decrease as x increases; and a ratio of greater than 1 indicates the odds of p increase as x increases. Variables are considered significant if they have a p-value of ≤.05.

*These findings are discussed in "Rate of Injury Among Victims of Intimate Partner Rape and Physical Assault."

4. *Ibid.*, Hornung, McCullough, and Sugimoto.

5. Hotaling, G.T., and D.B. Sugarman, "An Analysis of Risk Markers in Husband-to-Wife Violence," *Journal of Family Violence* 5 (1990): 1–13; Kaufman, K.G., J.L. Jasinski, and E. Aldarondo, "Sociocultural Status and Incidence of Marital Violence in Hispanic Families," *Violence and Victims* 9 (3) (1994): 207–222.

6. Frieze, I., and A. Browne, "Violence in Marriage," in *Family Violence,* eds. L. Ohlin and M. Tonry, Chicago: University of Chicago Press, 1989: 163–218; Levinson, D., *Violence in Cross-Cultural Perspective,* Newbury Park, California: Sage Publications, 1989.

7. Sobsey, D., *Violence and Abuse in the Lives of People With Disabilities: The End of Silent Acceptance?* Baltimore: Paul H. Brookes Publishing Company, 1994; Sobsey, D., and C. Varnhagen, "Sexual Abuse, Assault, and Exploitation of Individuals With Disabilities," *Child Sexual Abuse: Critical Perspectives on Prevention, Intervention, and Treatment,* eds. C. Gagley and R.J. Thomlinson, Toronto: Wall and Emerson, 1991: 203–216.

8. Johnson, M.P., "Patriarchal Terrorism and Common Couple Violence: Two Forms of Violence Against Women," *Journal of Marriage and the Family* 57 (1995): 283–294.

Point in Relationship When Violence Occurs

It is a common belief that the termination of a relationship poses an increased risk for, or escalation of, intimate partner violence. This assumption is based on two types of evidence: Divorced or separated women report more intimate partner violence than do married women.[1] Also, interviews with men who have killed their wives indicate that either threats of separation by their partner or actual separation are most often the precipitating events that lead to the murder.[2]

The NVAW Survey found that married women who lived apart from their husbands were nearly four times more likely to report that their husbands had raped, physically assaulted, and/or stalked them than were women who lived with their husbands (20 percent and 5.4 percent). Similarly, married men who lived apart from their wives were nearly three times more likely to report that their wives had victimized them than were men who lived with their wives (7.0 percent and 2.4 percent). These findings suggest

that termination of a relationship poses an increased risk of intimate partner violence for both women and men. However, it should be noted that the survey data do not indicate whether the violence happened before, after, or at the time the couple separated. Thus, it is unclear whether the separation triggered the violence or the violence triggered the separation.

To test the assumption that the termination of a relationship leads to an increased risk of intimate partner violence, the NVAW Survey asked women victimized by a former spouse or cohabiting partner whether their victimization occurred before, after, or both before and after the relationship ended. Only 6.3 percent of the rape victims and 4.2 percent of the physical assault victims said their victimization started after the relationship ended (exhibit 10). These findings suggest most rapes and physical assaults perpetrated against women by intimates occur in the context of an ongoing rather than terminated

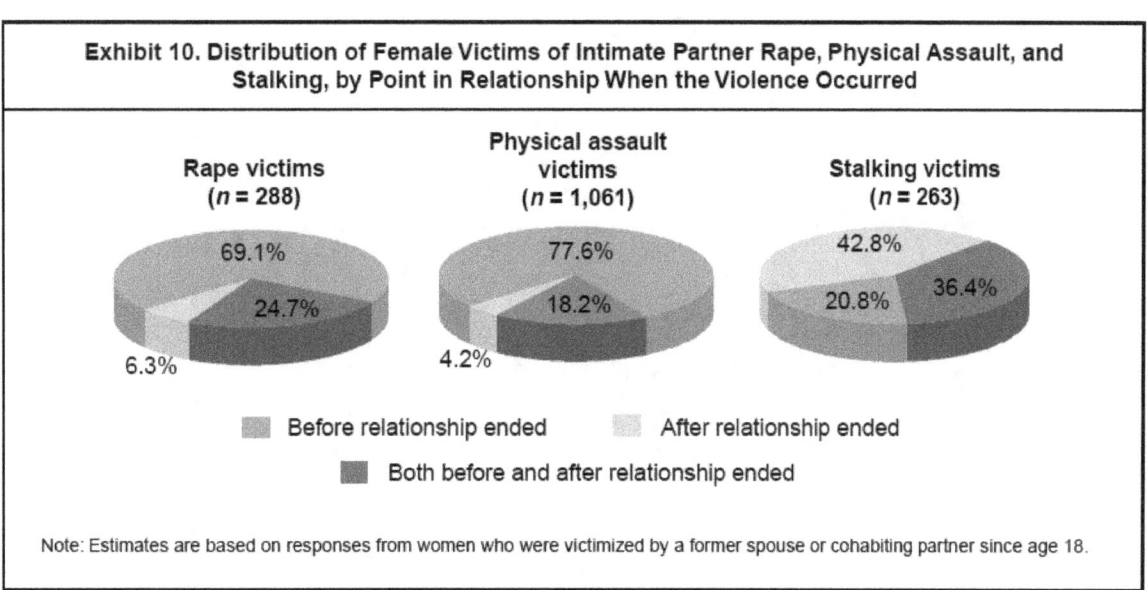

Exhibit 10. Distribution of Female Victims of Intimate Partner Rape, Physical Assault, and Stalking, by Point in Relationship When the Violence Occurred

Rape victims (*n* = 288): 69.1%, 24.7%, 6.3%
Physical assault victims (*n* = 1,061): 77.6%, 18.2%, 4.2%
Stalking victims (*n* = 263): 42.8%, 36.4%, 20.8%

Before relationship ended   After relationship ended
Both before and after relationship ended

Note: Estimates are based on responses from women who were victimized by a former spouse or cohabiting partner since age 18.

relationship. In comparison, 42.8 percent of the stalking victims said their victimization started after the relationship ended. Thus, stalking is more likely to occur in the context of a terminated relationship than is rape or physical assault.

It is not possible to ascertain from the data whether violence occurring before the relationship ended was linked to threats about leaving the relationship. It is also unclear whether women who said they were victimized before and after the relationship ended experienced more severe violence at the time of separation. Finally, it is important to note that when a relationship ends is a matter of interpretation rather than objective reality. Some women may have equated the end of the relationship with when they or their partner first started talking about leaving the relationship, whereas others may have equated it with the formal dissolution of a marriage. Clearly, more research is needed on how terminating a relationship increases the risk of intimate partner violence for women and men.

Notes

1. Klaus, P., and M. Rand, *Family Violence*, Special Report, Washington, D.C.: U.S. Department of Justice, Bureau of Justice Statistics, 1984, NCJ 093449; Stark, E., and A. Flitcraft, "Violence Among Intimates: An Epidemiological Review," in *Handbook of Family Violence,* ed. V.B. Van Hasselt, New York: Plenum Press, 1988: 307–308; Zawit, M.W., *Violence Between Intimates,* Washington, D.C.: U.S. Department of Justice, Bureau of Justice Statistics, 1994, NCJ 149259.

2. Bernard, M.L., and J.L. Bernard, "Violent Intimacy: The Family as a Model for Love Relationships," *Family Relations* 32 (1983): 283–286; Daly, M., and M. Wilson, "Evolutionary Social Psychology and Family Homicide," *Science* 242 (1988): 519–524.

Frequency and Duration of Intimate Partner Rape and Physical Assault

Results from the NVAW Survey confirm previous reports that much of the violence perpetrated against women by intimates is chronic in nature.[1] Approximately half (51.2 percent) of the women raped by an intimate and two-thirds (65.5 percent) of the women physically assaulted by an intimate said they were victimized multiple times by the same partner. (Stalking victims were not asked how many times they were stalked by the same partner because stalking by definition means repeated acts of threat and harassment.) Overall, female rape victims averaged 4.5 rapes by the same partner, and female physical assault victims averaged 6.9 assaults. Among women who were victimized multiple times by the same partner, 62.6 percent of the rape victims and 69.5 percent of the assault victims said their victimization lasted a year or more. On average, women who were raped multiple times said their victimization occurred over 3.8 years, and women who were physically assaulted multiple times said their victimization occurred over 4.5 years (exhibit 11).

The survey also found that much of the violence perpetrated against men by intimates is chronic in nature. Two-thirds (66.2 percent) of the physically assaulted men said they were assaulted more than once by the same intimate partner. Of these, 66.2 percent said their victimization lasted a year or more. On average, male victims of intimate partner physical assault reported 4.4 assaults by the same partner. On average, men

Exhibit 11. Distribution of Rape and Physical Assault Victims, by Frequency and Duration of Victimization and Gender[a]			
	Rape Victims (%)	Physical Assault Victims (%)	
Frequency/Duration of Victimization	Women	Women	Men
Number of times victimized by the same partner	(n = 373)	(n = 1,229)	(n = 517)
1	48.8	34.5	33.8
2–9	36.0	45.7	55.6
10 or more	15.2	19.8	10.6
Average number of times victimized[b]	4.5 (0.4)	6.9[c] (0.4)	4.4 (0.3)
Number of years victimized by the same partner[d]	(n = 187)	(n = 794)	(n = 337)
Less than 1	37.4	30.5	33.8
1–5	39.5	42.9	43.7
More than 5	23.1	26.6	22.5
Average number of years victimized[b]	3.8 (0.4)	4.5[c] (0.2)	3.6 (0.3)

[a]Estimates are based on responses from women and men victimized by an intimate since age 18. Estimates not calculated for male rape victims because there were fewer than five victims when stratified by variables.

[b]Numbers in parentheses are standard errors of the mean.

[c]Differences between women and men are statistically different: Student's t.

[d]Estimates are based on responses from women and men assaulted multiple times by the same intimate.

reporting multiple assaults said their victimization lasted 3.6 years (exhibit 11). Although much of the physical assault perpetrated against men by intimates is chronic, it is important to note that both the average frequency and the average duration of physical assaults perpetrated against women by intimates are significantly higher than the average frequency/duration of physical assaults perpetrated against men by intimates.

(Estimates were not calculated for male rape victims because there were fewer than five victims when stratified by variables.)

Note

1. Langen, P.A., and C.A. Innes, *Preventing Domestic Violence Against Women,* Special Report, Washington, D.C.: U.S. Department of Justice, Bureau of Justice Statistics, 1986, NCJ 102037.

Rate of Injury Among Victims of Intimate Partner Rape and Physical Assault

To generate information on the extent and nature of injuries associated with violent victimization, respondents disclosing rape and physical assault were asked whether they were injured during their most recent victimization and, if so, the types of injuries they sustained. (Respondents disclosing stalking victimization were not asked these questions because the definition of stalking used in the survey does not include behaviors that inflict physical harm.)

The survey found that 36.2 percent of the women raped by an intimate since age 18 sustained an injury other than the rape itself during their most recent victimization. (Estimates were not calculated for male rape victims because there were fewer than five victims when stratified by variables.) The survey also found that women physically assaulted by an intimate were more than twice as likely as their male counterparts (41.5 percent and 19.9 percent, respectively) to be

	Rape Victims (%)	Physical Assault Victims (%)	
Injury/Medical Care	Women	Women	Men
Was victim injured?	(*n* = 439)	(*n* = 1,451)	(*n* = 542)
Yes	36.2	41.5[b]	19.9
No	63.8	58.5	80.1
Did injured victim receive medical care?[c]	(*n* = 158)	(*n* = 598)	(*n* = 107)
Yes	31.0	28.1	21.5
No	69.0	71.9	78.5
Type of medical care received[d]	(*n* = 49)	(*n* = 168)	(*n* = 23)
Hospital	79.6	78.6	82.6
Physician	59.2	51.8	43.5
Dental	18.4[e]	9.5	—[f]
Ambulance/paramedic	20.4	14.9	—[f]
Physical therapy	22.4	8.9	—[f]
Type of hospital care received[g]	(*n* = 39)	(*n* = 132)	(*n* = 19)
Emergency room	51.3	59.1	63.2
Outpatient	30.8	24.2	—[f]
Overnight	17.9[e]	16.7	—[f]

Exhibit 12. Distribution of Intimate Partner Rape and Physical Assault Victims, by Injury, Type of Medical Care Received, and Gender[a]

Note: Total percentages for type of medical and hospital care received exceed 100 percent because some victims had multiple forms of medical/hospital care.

[a] Estimates are based on the most recent intimate partner rape/physical assault since age 18. Estimates were not calculated for male rape victims because there were fewer than five victims when stratified by variables.

[b] Differences between women and men are statistically significant: χ^2, $p \leq .001$.

[c] Estimates are based on responses from injured victims.

[d] Estimates are based on responses from victims who received medical care.

[e] Relative standard error exceeds 30 percent.

[f] Estimates were not calculated on fewer than five individuals.

[g] Estimates are based on responses from victims who received hospital care.

injured during their most recent victimization (exhibit 12). This finding supports previous research that shows women are more likely than men to be injured during an assault by an intimate.[1]

Injury estimates for female victims of intimate partner violence generated by the NVAW Survey are somewhat lower than injury estimates generated by the NCVS. A recent study conducted by the Bureau of Justice Statistics found that 51 percent of the assaults perpetrated against women by intimates during 1992–96 resulted in some type of injury to the victim.[2] The higher rate of injury uncovered by the NCVS suggests that the context in which that study is administered and the type of screening questions used leads respondents to report more serious types of assaults to interviewers.

Most of the women who were injured during their most recent intimate partner rape or physical assault sustained relatively minor injuries, such as scratches, bruises, and welts. Relatively few women sustained more serious types of injuries, such as lacerations, broken bones, dislocated

joints, head or spinal cord injuries, chipped or broken teeth, or internal injuries (exhibit 13).

Risk factors associated with injury

Logistic regression was used to determine what characteristics of the victim, perpetrator, and incident may increase the risk of injury during intimate partner rapes and physical assaults. Separate regressions, using a backward stepwise procedure, were conducted for female victims of intimate partner rape ($n = 374$), female victims of intimate partner physical assault ($n = 1,254$), and male victims of intimate partner physical assault ($n = 479$).

In each of the regressions, the dependent variable was whether the victim was injured during her or his most recent victimization by an intimate. The independent variables were as follows:

- Whether the perpetrator was a spouse, cohabiting partner, or date.

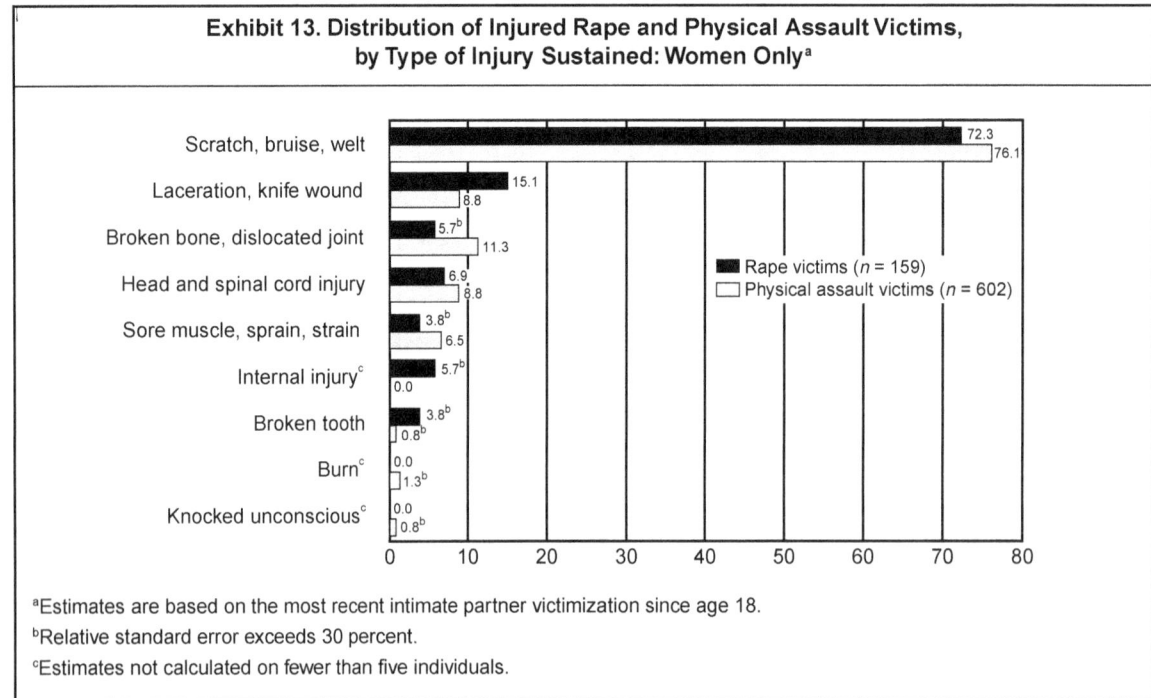

Exhibit 13. Distribution of Injured Rape and Physical Assault Victims, by Type of Injury Sustained: Women Only[a]

[a]Estimates are based on the most recent intimate partner victimization since age 18.
[b]Relative standard error exceeds 30 percent.
[c]Estimates not calculated on fewer than five individuals.

- Whether the victim was white, African-American, American Indian/Alaska Native, Asian/Pacific Islander, or mixed race.

- Whether the victim was Hispanic.

- Whether the victim was 18 to 25 years of age.

- Whether the incident occurred in the victim's or perpetrator's home.

- Whether the perpetrator threatened to harm or kill the victim or someone close to the victim.

- Whether the perpetrator used a weapon.

- Whether the victim was using drugs or alcohol at the time of the incident.

- Whether the perpetrator was using drugs or alcohol at the time of the incident.

Results of the logistic regression show that women raped by an intimate partner were significantly more likely to be injured if they were Hispanic, if their perpetrator was a spouse or cohabiting partner (rather than a date), if their perpetrator threatened to harm or kill them or someone close to them, and if their perpetrator was using drugs or alcohol at the time of the incident (see table III in sidebar, "Results of the Logistic Regressions" in "Risk Factors Associated With Intimate Partner Violence").

In comparison, women who were physically assaulted by an intimate partner were significantly more likely to be injured if their perpetrator threatened to harm or kill them or someone close to them and if the perpetrator was using drugs or alcohol at the time of the incident (see table IV in sidebar, "Results of the Logistic Regressions" in "Risk Factors Associated With Intimate Partner Violence").

Finally, results of the logistic regression show that men who were physically assaulted by an intimate partner were significantly more likely to be injured if their perpetrator threatened to harm or kill them or someone close to them and if their perpetrator used a weapon (see table V in sidebar, "Results of the Logistic Regressions" in "Risk Factors Associated With Intimate Partner Violence").

Results of the logistic regressions show a strong link between threats of bodily injury and actual occurrences of injury. These findings imply that threats of violence should be taken seriously, and violence prevention strategies should emphasize this fact. Results also show a strong link between drug and alcohol use on the part of the perpetrator and victim injury. These findings suggest that some of the inhibitors that may prevent persons from hurting others under ordinary circumstances are relaxed when persons are under the influence of drugs or alcohol.

Notes

1. Brush, L.D., "Violent Acts and Injurious Outcomes in Married Couples: Methodological Issues in the National Survey of Family and Households," *Gender and Society* 4 (1) (1990): 56–67; Kurz, D., "Interventions With Battered Women in Health Care Settings," *Violence and Victims,* 5 (1990): 243–256; Langen, P.A., and C.A. Innes, *Preventing Domestic Violence Against Women,* Special Report, Washington, D.C.: U.S. Department of Justice, Bureau of Justice Statistics, 1986, NCJ 102037; McLeer, S.R., and R. Anwar, "A Study of Battered Women Presenting in Emergency Departments," *American Journal of Public Health* 79 (1989): 65–66; Morse, B., "Beyond the Conflict Tactics Scale: Assessing Gender Differences in Partner Violence," *Violence and Victims* 10 (4) (1995): 251–272; Schwartz, M.D., "Gender and Injury in Spousal Assault," *Sociological Focus* 20 (1987): 61–75; Stark, E., A. Flitcraft, and W. Frazier, "Medicine and Patriarchal Violence: The Social Construction of a 'Private' Event," *International Journal of Health Services* 9 (1979): 461–493.

2. Greenfeld, L., M.R. Rand, D. Craven, P.A. Klaus, C.A. Perkins, C. Ringel, G. Warchol, C. Matson, and J.A. Fox, *Violence by Intimates: Analysis of Data on Crimes by Current or Former Spouses, Boyfriends, and Girlfriends*, Bureau of Justice Statistics Factbook, Washington, D.C.: U.S. Department of Justice, Bureau of Justice Statistics, 1998, NCJ 167237.

Victims' Use of Medical Services

Approximately one-third (31 percent) of the women injured during their most recent intimate partner rape received some type of medical care (e.g., ambulance/paramedic services, care in a hospital emergency facility, physical therapy). Somewhat fewer women and men who were injured during their most recent physical assault received some type of medical care (28.1 percent and 21.5 percent, respectively) (exhibit 12). Injured women and men had similar rates and types of medical care. This indicates that injuries sustained by women and men were similar in severity.

Some victims received more than one type of medical care (e.g., hospitalization as well as outpatient physical therapy), whereas others received a specific type of medical care more than once (e.g., 13 physical therapy sessions). Thus, the annual number of medical treatments provided to intimate partner rape and physical assault victims exceeds the annual number of intimate partner victimizations that resulted in treatment.

Estimates of medical services utilization

Exhibit 14 provides estimates of the average number of nights spent in the hospital and the average number of visits made to specific medical providers by adult victims of intimate partner rape and physical assault. These estimates are based on responses from victims who received the specific type of medical care considered. For example, the estimate of the average number of nights spent in the hospital by female intimate partner rape victims (3.9) is based only on responses by female intimate partner rape victims treated in a hospital on an inpatient basis. Some of the average frequency estimates are based on a very small number of responses and, therefore, have a relatively high margin of error (see footnotes c through f in exhibit 14).

Exhibit 14. Average Number of Medical Care Visits for Intimate Partner Rape and Physical Assault Victims, by Type of Medical Care and Gender[a]			
	Rape Victims	Physical Assault Victims	
Type of Medical Care	Women[b]	Women[c]	Men[d]
Emergency room visit	1.9	1.9	1.1
Outpatient visit	1.6	3.1	—[e]
Overnight in hospital	3.9[f]	5.7	—[e]
Physician visit	5.2	3.2	2.0
Dental visit	2.3	4.4	—[e]
Ambulance/paramedic visit	1.3	1.1	—[e]
Physical therapy visit	13.4[f]	21.1[f]	—[e]

Note: Estimates are based on responses from victims who received the specific type of medical treatment considered.

[a]Estimates are based on the most recent intimate partner rape/physical assault since age 18. Estimates not calculated for male rape victims because there were fewer than five victims when stratified by variables.

[b]The standard error of the mean for each estimate in this column is 0.5, 0.3, 1.3, 1.2, 0.4, 0.2, and 5.1, respectively.

[c]The standard error of the mean for each estimate in this column is 0.3, 0.7, 1.7, 0.5, 1.3, 0.1, and 8.7, respectively.

[d]The standard error of the mean for each estimate in this column is 0.1, —[e], —[e], 0.3, —[e], —[e], and —[e], respectively.

[e]Estimates not calculated on fewer than five individuals.

[f]Relative standard error exceeds 30 percent.

Exhibit 15. Average Annual Injury and Medical Utilization Estimates for Adult Victims of Intimate Partner Rape and Physical Assault, by Gender			
	Estimated Number of Victimizations and Visits per Year		
	Rape Victims[a]	Physical Assault Victims	
	Women	Women	Men
Victimization	322,230	4,450,807	2,921,562
Victimization resulting in injury	116,647	1,847,085	581,391
Victimization resulting in medical care	36,161	519,031	124,999
Victimization resulting in:			
Hospital care	28,784	407,958	103,249
Physician care	21,407	268,858	54,375
Dental care	6,654	49,308	—[b]
Ambulance/paramedic care	7,377	77,336	—[b]
Physical therapy	8,100	46,194	—[b]
Victimization resulting in hospital:			
Emergency room care	14,766	241,103	65,253
Outpatient care	8,865	98,726	—[b]
Overnight care	5,152	68,129	—[b]
Total number of:			
Emergency room visits	28,055	458,096	71,778
Outpatient visits	14,184	306,051	—[b]
Overnights in hospital	20,093	388,335	—[b]
Physician visits	111,316	860,346	108,750
Dental visits	15,304	216,955	—[b]
Ambulance/paramedic visits	9,590	85,070	—[b]
Physical therapy visits	108,540	974,693	—[b]

[a] All relative standard errors in this column exceed 30 percent.

[b] Estimates not calculated on fewer than five individuals.

Exhibit 15 presents estimates of the number of intimate partner rapes and physical assaults resulting in injuries annually, as well as estimates of the specific types of medical care provided for these rapes and physical assaults annually. The first row of estimates is based on reported incidents of intimate partner violence in the past 12 months (see exhibit 2). The remaining estimates are based on the most recent intimate partner victimization since age 18 (see exhibits 12 and 14). As these estimates show, women and men made 557,929 visits to hospital emergency rooms for injuries sustained during rapes and physical assaults perpetrated by intimate partners in the year preceding the survey. Fully 87 percent (486,151) of these visits were made by

women. These findings support results from previous studies that show a significant number of women who have experienced intimate partner violence are seen in hospital emergency rooms.[1]

The NVAW Survey estimate of women and men treated by hospital emergency department personnel is substantially higher than an estimate generated from the Study of Injured Victims of Violence (SIVV), a hospital record-extraction study conducted for the Bureau of Justice Statistics by the Consumer Product Safety Commission. The SIVV found that, during 1994, hospital emergency department personnel treated an estimated 243,400 women and men for injuries sustained at the hands of spouses, ex-spouses, boyfriends, and girlfriends.[2] Included in the SIVV estimate (but excluded from the NVAW Survey estimate) is hospital emergency department care to child and adolescent victims of intimate partner violence, male victims of intimate partner rape, and male and female victims of intimate partner sexual assault and robbery. Because these groups were excluded from the NVAW Survey estimates, differences between the two studies' estimates are even larger than they appear. However, the SIVV could not identify the patient/offender relationship in 28.8 percent (407,600) of the hospital emergency department visits identified by the study. If just half of these visits were to victims of intimate partner violence, NVAW Survey and SIVV estimates would be more similar.

Notes

1. Abbott, J., R. Johnson, J. Koziol-McLain, and S.R. Lowenstein, "Domestic Violence Against Women: Incidence and Prevalence in an Emergency Department," *Journal of the American Medical Association* 273 (1995): 1763–1767; Dearwater, S.R., J.H. Coben, J.C. Campbell, G. Nash, N. Glass, E. McLoughlin, and B. Bekemeier, "Prevalence of Intimate Partner Abuse in Women Treated at Community Hospital Emergency Departments," *Journal of the American Medical Association* 280 (5) (1998): 433–438; McLeer, S.R., and R. Anwar, "A Study of Battered Women Presenting in Emergency Departments," *American Journal of Public Health* 79 (1989): 65–66.

2. Rand, M.R., *Violence-Related Injuries Treated in Hospital Emergency Departments,* Special Report, Washington, D.C.: U.S. Department of Justice, Bureau of Justice Statistics, 1997, NCJ 156921.

Victims' Involvement With the Justice System

Reporting to the police

Less than one-fifth (17.2 percent) of the women raped by an intimate said their most recent rape was reported to the police. Thus, of the estimated 322,230 intimate partner rapes perpetrated against U.S. women in the 12 months preceding the survey, only 55,424 were reported to law enforcement. (The 322,230 estimate is based on responses from 16 women and should

therefore be viewed with caution.) The vast majority of the reported rapes were reported within 24 hours. Most of the reports were made by the victim, rather than a friend, relative, or other third party (exhibit 16).

The survey found that women who were physically assaulted by an intimate were significantly more likely than their male counterparts to report their victimization to the police (26.7 percent and

Law Enforcement Outcome	Rape Victims (%)	Physical Assault Victims (%)		Stalking Victims (%)	
	Women	Women	Men	Women	Men
Victimization reported to police	(n = 441)	(n = 1,149)	(n = 541)	(n = 343)	(n = 47)
Reported	17.2	26.7[b]	13.5	51.9[b]	36.2
Not reported	82.8	73.3	86.5	48.1	63.8
Timing of report	(n = 75)	(n = 370)	(n = 73)	(n = 174)	(n = 15)
Within 24 hours	92.0	94.0	91.7	78.7	80.0
After 24 hours	8.0[c]	6.0	8.3[c]	21.3	—[d]
Reporter identity[e]	(n = 75)	(n = 370)	(n = 73)	(n = 179)	(n = 16)
Victim	78.7	78.4[b]	65.3	92.2	87.5
Other person	21.3	21.6	34.7	7.8[c]	—[d]
Police response[e, f]	(n = 75)	(n = 370)	(n = 73)	(n = 178)	(n = 17)
Took report	77.6	76.2[b]	64.4	67.4	64.7
Arrested or detained attacker	47.4	36.4[b]	12.3	28.7	—[d]
Referred victim to prosecutor or court	10.5[c]	33.9	23.3	28.1	—[d]
Referred victim to services	—[d]	25.1	17.8	21.3	—[d]
Gave victim advice on self-protective measures	—[d]	26.1	17.8	23.1	35.3[c]
Did nothing	—[d]	11.1[c]	19.2	18.5	—[d]

Exhibit 16. Distribution of Intimate Partner Rape, Physical Assault, and Stalking Victims, by Law Enforcement Outcomes and Gender[a]

[a]Estimates are based on the most recent intimate partner victimization since age 18. Estimates not calculated for male rape victims because there were fewer than five victims when stratified by variables.
[b]Differences between women and men are statistically significant: χ^2, $p \le .05$.
[c]Relative standard error exceeds 30 percent; statistical tests not performed.
[d]Estimates not calculated for fewer than five victims.
[e]Estimates are based on responses from victims whose victimization was reported to the police.
[f]Estimates exceed 100 percent because some victims reported multiple police responses.

Exhibit 17. Distribution of Rape, Physical Assault, and Stalking Victims Who Did Not Report Their Victimization to the Police, by Reasons for Not Reporting and Gender[a]

Reason for Not Reporting[b]	Rape Victims (%)	Physical Assault Victims (%)		Stalking Victims (%)	
	Women (n = 311)	Women (n = 2,062)	Men (n = 468)	Women (n = 165)	Men (n = 30)
Police couldn't do anything	13.2	99.7	100.0	100.0	100.0
Police wouldn't believe me	7.1	61.3[c]***	45.1	98.2	93.3
Fear of perpetrator	21.2	11.7[c]	1.9[d]	38.2[c]**	16.7[d]
Minor, one-time incident	20.3	37.9[c]***	58.5	33.9	36.7[d]
Ashamed, wanted to keep incident private	16.1	10.4[c]**	7.1	61.8	76.7
Wanted to handle it myself	7.7	7.3	5.8	7.9	—[e]
Victim or attacker moved away	—[e]	2.4	—[e]	12.1	—[e]
Attacker was a police officer	—[e]	4.7	3.8	7.9	—[e]
Too young, a child	3.5	2.2	1.5[d]	—[e]	—[e]
Reported to the military or someone else	—[e]	0.8[d]	—[e]	—[e]	—[e]
Didn't want police, court involvement	5.8	32.0[c]**	24.6	35.2	40.0
Wanted to protect attacker, relationship, or children	8.7	34.8[c]**	29.5	45.5	43.3

[a]Estimates are based on the most recent intimate partner victimization since age 18. Estimates not calculated for male rape victims because there were fewer than five victims when stratified by variables.

[b]Estimates exceed 100 percent because some victims gave multiple responses.

[c]Differences between women and men are statistically significant: χ^2, ***$p \leq .001$, **$p \leq .05$.

[d]Relative standard error exceeds 30 percent; statistical tests not performed.

[e]Estimates not calculated for fewer than five victims.

13.5 percent, respectively). Similarly, female victims of intimate partner stalking were significantly more likely than their male counterparts to report their victimization to the police (51.9 percent and 36.2 percent, respectively) (exhibit 16). As with reports of intimate partner rape, most of the physical assault and stalking reports were made within 24 hours of the incident, and most were made by the victim.

Police response to reports of intimate partner violence

Survey findings confirm that the majority of reports of intimate partner violence made to the police result in an officer taking a statement, that is, conducting a face-to-face interview with the victim (exhibit 16). The survey found no evidence that police respond differently to women than men stalked by an intimate. However, there is some evidence that police respond differently to women than men who are physically assaulted by an intimate. A comparison of police responses to reports of physical assault committed against women and men by intimates showed that police were significantly more likely to take a report and to arrest or detain the perpetrator if the victim was female (exhibit 16). Although it is unclear from the survey data why police respond differently to reports of physical assaults involving female than male victims, it is possible they do so because physical assaults committed against women tend to be more chronic and more injurious. (See "Frequency and Duration of Intimate Partner Rape and Physical Assaults" and "Rate of Injury Among Victims of Intimate Partner Rape and Physical Assault.")

Reasons for not reporting victimization to the police

When asked why they chose not to report their victimization to the police, approximately one-fifth (21.2 percent) of the female rape victims said they were afraid their attacker would retaliate, and one-fifth (20.3 percent) said the rape was a one-time or minor incident. In addition, 16 percent reported they were too ashamed or wanted to keep the incident private, and 13 percent said the police could not do anything (exhibit 17).

When asked why they chose not to report their victimization to the police, nearly all of the physical assault victims said they did not think the police could do anything about their victimization, whereas 61.5 percent of the women and 45 percent of the men said the police would not have believed them. In addition, approximately one-third of the women and one-quarter of the men said they did not want the police or courts

involved (exhibit 17). These findings suggest that many victims of intimate partner violence—men and women alike—do not consider the justice system a viable or appropriate intervention at the time of their victimization.

Note that significantly more women than men chose not to report their physical assault to the police because they were afraid of their attacker, whereas significantly more men than women chose not to report their physical assault to the police because they considered it a minor or one-time incident. These findings underscore the fact that violence committed against women by intimates tends to be more threatening and severe than violence committed against men by intimates.

The survey found no significant differences between women's and men's reasons for not reporting their stalking to the police. However, these findings should be viewed with caution given the small number of male victims (exhibit 17).

Exhibit 18. Distribution of Intimate Partner Rape, Physical Assault, and Stalking Victims, by Prosecution Outcomes and Gender[a]					
	Rape Victims (%)	Physical Assault Victims (%)		Stalking Victims (%)	
Prosecution Outcome	Women	Women	Men	Women	Men
Perpetrator was prosecuted	(n = 439)	(n = 1,436)	(n = 544)	(n = 336)	(n = 47)
Yes	7.5	7.3	1.1[b]	14.6	—[c]
No	92.5	92.7	98.9	85.4	93.6
Perpetrator was convicted[d]	(n = 31)	(n = 96)	(n < 5)	(n = 40)	(n < 5)
Yes	41.9	47.9	—[c]	40.0	—[c]
No	58.1	52.1	—[c]	60.0	—[c]
Perpetrator was sentenced to jail or prison[e]	(n = 13)	(n = 45)	(n < 5)	(n = 16)	(n < 5)
Yes	69.2	35.6	—[c]	56.3	—[c]
No	—[c]	64.4	—[c]	47.1	—[c]

[a]Estimates are based on the most recent intimate partner victimization since age 18. Estimates not calculated for male rape victims because there were fewer than five victims when stratified by variables.
[b]Relative standard error exceeds 30 percent; statistical tests not performed.
[c]Estimates not calculated for fewer than five victims.
[d]Estimates are based on responses from victims whose perpetrator was prosecuted.
[e]Estimates are based on responses from victims whose perpetrator was convicted.

Criminal prosecution

Information from the NVAW Survey shows that violence perpetrated against women by intimates is rarely prosecuted. Only 7.5 percent of the women who were raped by an intimate, 7.3 percent of the women who were physically assaulted by an intimate, and 14.6 percent of the women who were stalked by an intimate said their attacker was criminally prosecuted (exhibit 18). These figures increase to 31.1 percent, 24.7 percent, and 25.4 percent, respectively (not shown in exhibit 18), when only victims whose stalking was reported to the police are considered. According to women's perceptions of the outcome of the prosecution, less than one-half of the intimate partner perpetrators who had criminal charges filed against them were convicted of a crime (exhibit 18).

The number of victims ($n < 5$) was insufficient to reliably calculate prosecution estimates for male victims of intimate partner rape or stalking. However, prosecution estimates for male victims of physical assault show that violence committed against men by intimates is even less likely to be criminally prosecuted than violence committed against women by intimates. Only 1.1 percent of the men who were physically assaulted by an intimate since the age of 18 said their attacker was criminally prosecuted (exhibit 18). This figure increases to 4.1 percent when only victims whose physical assault was reported to the police are considered.

Temporary restraining orders

The survey found that female victims of intimate partner violence were significantly more likely than their male counterparts to obtain a protective or restraining order against their assailant. Specifically, 17.1 percent of the women but only 3.5 percent of the men who were physically assaulted by an intimate obtained a restraining order against their assailant after their most recent victimization. Similarly, 36.6 percent of the women but only 17 percent of the men who were stalked by an intimate obtained a restraining order against their assailant (exhibit 19). These findings suggest that women are more frightened by intimates who victimize them. They also underscore the fact that violence committed against women by intimates is more chronic and severe than violence committed against men by intimates.

	Rape Victims (%)	Physical Assault Victims (%)		Stalking Victims (%)	
Exhibit 19. Distribution of Intimate Partner Rape, Physical Assault, and Stalking Victims, by Protective Order Outcomes and Gender[a]					
Protective Order Outcome	Women	Women	Men	Women	Men
Victim obtained a temporary restraining order (TRO)	(n = 433)	(n = 1,420)	(n = 544)	(n = 333)	(n = 47)
Yes	16.4	17.1[b]	3.5	36.6	17.0[c]
No	83.6	82.9	96.5	63.4	83.0
TRO was violated[d]	(n = 71)	(n = 239)	(n = 19)	(n = 122)	(n = 8)
Yes	67.6	50.6	68.4	69.7	87.5
No	32.4	49.4	31.6[c]	30.3	—[e]

[a]Estimates are based on the most recent intimate partner victimization since age 18. Estimates not calculated for male rape victims because there were fewer than five victims when stratified by variables.

[b]Differences between women and men are statistically significant: χ^2, $p \leq .001$.

[c]Relative standard error exceeds 30 percent; statistical tests not performed.

[d]Estimates are based on responses from victims who obtained a TRO.

[e]Estimates not calculated for fewer than five victims.

Exhibit 20. Average Annual Justice System Utilization Estimates for Adult Victims of Intimate Partner Rape, Physical Assault, and Stalking, by Gender					
	Estimated Number of Victimizations per Year				
	Rape Victims	Physical Assault Victims		Stalking Victims	
	Women[a]	Women	Men	Women	Men
Total victimization	322,230	4,450,807	2,921,562	503,485	185,496
Victimization with:					
Report to police	55,424	1,188,365	394,411	261,309	67,150
Arrest of perpetrator	26,271	432,565	48,513	74,996	15,780
Criminal prosecution	24,167	324,909	17,529	67,467	—[b]
Conviction	10,126	155,631	—[b]	26,986	—[b]
Jail/prison sentence	7,007	55,405	—[b]	15,193	—[b]
Temporary restraining order (TRO)	52,846	761,088	102,255	184,276	31,534
TRO violation	35,724	385,111	69,942	128,440	27,592

[a]All relative standard errors in this column exceed 30 percent.
[b]Estimates not calculated for fewer than five victims.

The survey also found that women who were stalked by an intimate were significantly more likely to obtain a restraining order against their assailant than were women who were physically assaulted or raped by an intimate. Similarly, men who were stalked by an intimate were significantly more likely to obtain a restraining order than were men who were physically assaulted. A recent study by the American Bar Association may help explain these findings. The study found that victims of violence rarely seek restraining orders as a form of early intervention but rather as an act of desperation after they have experienced extensive problems.[1] Because stalking by definition involves repeated acts of harassment and threats, stalking victims were more likely than rape or physical assault victims to have experienced extensive problems and to have felt a sense of desperation.

Information from the survey confirms previous reports that most temporary restraining orders are violated.[2] More than two-thirds of the restraining orders obtained by women against intimates who raped or stalked them were violated, and approximately one-half of the orders obtained by women against intimates who physi-cally assaulted them were violated. Similarly, more than two-thirds of the restraining orders obtained by men against intimates who physically assaulted them and nearly nine-tenths of the orders obtained by men against intimates who stalked them were violated (exhibit 19).

Estimates of justice system utilization

Exhibit 20 presents estimates of the number of intimate partner rape, physical assault, and stalking victimizations that result in a report to the police, an arrest, a criminal filing, a conviction, and a temporary restraining order annually. The first row of estimates is based on reported incidents of intimate partner violence in the past 12 months (see exhibit 2). The remaining estimates are based on the most recent intimate partner victimization since age 18 (see exhibits 16, 18, and 19). According to these estimates, law enforcement personnel receive 1,966,659 reports of intimate partner rape, physical assault, and stalking annually. It is unclear from the data how police personnel classify these reports. For example, police may classify some physical assault reports as threats or intimidation, and they may classify some stalking cases as trespassing or vandalism.

According to NVAW Survey estimates, law enforcement personnel arrest or detain 598,125 suspects of intimate partner rape, physical assault, and stalking annually, and 434,072 such suspects are criminally prosecuted annually. It is unclear how many of these suspects are charged with misdemeanor versus felony crimes. It is also unclear what specific types of charges are filed against these suspects (e.g., simple versus aggravated assault, stalking, harassment).

Survey estimates show that 1,131,999 victims of intimate partner rape, physical assault, and stalking obtain protective or restraining orders against their attackers annually. Approximately 60 percent (646,809) of these orders are violated.

Notes

1. American Bar Association, *Legal Interventions in Family Violence: Research Findings and Policy Implications,* Research Report, Washington, D.C.: U.S. Department of Justice, Bureau of Justice Statistics, 1998, NCJ 171666.

2. *Ibid.* The ABA study found that 60 percent of the women with temporary restraining orders reported the order was violated within the year after it was issued.

Policy Implications

The NVAW Survey provides compelling evidence of the prevalence, incidence, and consequences of intimate partner violence in the United States. Information generated from the survey and presented in this report also addresses many controversial issues surrounding intimate partner violence research, such as whether women and men suffer equal rates of violence at the hands of intimate partners, whether race and Hispanic origin affect one's risk of intimate partner violence, and whether violence is more prevalent among same-sex cohabitants compared with heterosexual cohabitants. Thus, information presented in this report can help inform policy and intervention directed at violence perpetrated against women and men by intimate partners. Based on findings from the survey, the following conclusions can be drawn.

1. Intimate partner violence should be treated as a significant social problem. Analysis of the survey data validates previous research that shows intimate partner violence is a pervasive and serious social problem in the United States. According to survey estimates, approximately 1.5 million U.S. women and 834,732 U.S. men are raped and/or physically assaulted by an intimate partner annually. Because many of these victims suffer multiple victimizations, the number of intimate partner rapes and physical assaults perpetrated annually exceeds the number of intimate partner victims annually. Thus, an estimated 322,230 rapes and 4.5 million physical assaults are committed against U.S. women by intimate partners annually, and an estimated 2.9 million physical assaults are committed against U.S. men by intimate partners annually. [The estimated number of rapes perpetrated against U.S. women annually is based on 16 women who reported being raped by an intimate partner in the

12 months preceding the survey and should be viewed with caution. Furthermore, the number of male victims was insufficient ($n < 5$) to calculate the number of intimate partner rapes committed against men annually.] In addition, 503,485 U.S. women and 185,496 U.S. men are stalked by intimates annually. Given the pervasiveness of intimate partner rapes, physical assaults, and stalkings committed against women and men annually, it is imperative that intimate partner violence be treated as a major criminal justice and public health concern.

2. Women report significantly more intimate partner violence than do men. The survey found that women were significantly more likely than men to report being victimized by an intimate partner whether the type of violence was rape, physical assault, or stalking and whether the period was the victim's lifetime or the 12 months preceding the survey. Moreover, women who were physically assaulted by an intimate partner averaged significantly more assaults and suffered significantly more injuries than did their male counterparts. Given these findings, intimate partner violence should be considered first and foremost a crime against women, and prevention strategies should reflect this fact.

3. Studies are needed to determine why different national surveys have produced such disparate findings with respect to women's and men's experiences with intimate partner violence. Prior to the NVAW Survey, national information on women's and men's annual experiences with physical assault by an intimate came primarily from the Bureau of Justice Statistics' NCVS and the NFVS. The NVAW Survey finding that women report significantly more intimate partner violence than do men is consistent with findings from the NCVS but inconsistent with findings from the NFVS. Although the NVAW Survey and the NFVS used similar behaviorally specific questions to screen respondents for physical assault, victimization estimates generated from the NVAW Survey are substantially lower than those generated from the NFVS. Conversely, NVAW Survey victimization estimates are substantially higher than those generated from the NCVS. Studies are needed to determine how methodological differences, such as the context in which the survey is administered and question wording, affect women's and men's reporting of intimate partner violence.

4. Studies are needed to determine why the prevalence of intimate partner violence varies significantly among women of different racial and ethnic backgrounds. The survey found that American Indian/Alaska Native women report significantly more intimate partner rapes than do women from other racial backgrounds, and Asian/Pacific Islander women report significantly fewer intimate partner physical assaults. In addition, Hispanic women report significantly more intimate partner rapes than do non-Hispanic women. However, differences between minority groups diminish when certain demographic and relationship variables are controlled.

It is unclear from the survey data whether differences in intimate partner victimization rates among women of different racial and ethnic groups are caused by differences in reporting practices. It is also unclear how social, environmental, and demographic factors intersect with race and ethnicity to produce differences in intimate partner victimization rates among women of different racial and ethnic backgrounds. Thus, more research is needed to establish the degree of variance in the prevalence of intimate partner violence among women (and men) of diverse racial and ethnic groups and to determine how much of the variance may be explained by differences in such factors as cultural attitudes, community services, and income. Research is also needed to determine whether differences exist in intimate partner victimization rates for women of diverse

Asian/Pacific Islander groups, American Indian tribes, and Alaska Native communities. Finally, research is needed to determine whether differences exist in intimate partner victimization rates among minority women born in the United States and those who have recently immigrated.

5. Intimate partner violence is more prevalent among male same-sex couples than female same-sex couples. Findings from the NVAW Survey refute earlier findings that same-sex couples are about as violent as heterosexual couples. Male same-sex cohabitants were more likely to report victimization by a male partner than were male opposite-sex cohabitants by a female partner. In comparison, female same-sex cohabitants reported less violence by a female partner than did female heterosexual cohabitants by a male partner. These findings suggest that gay male couples are more violent than lesbian couples, whereas lesbian couples are less violent than heterosexual couples. These findings also indicate that intimate partner violence is perpetrated primarily by men, whether against same-sex or opposite-sex partners.

6. Violence and emotionally abusive and controlling behavior in intimate relationships are interrelated. The NVAW Survey provides compelling evidence of the link between violence and emotionally abusive and controlling behavior in intimate relationships. Women whose partners verbally abused them, were jealous or possessive, or denied them access to family, friends, and family income were significantly more likely to report being raped, physically assaulted, and/or stalked by their partners, even when sociodemographic factors such as race and education were controlled. These findings suggest that many women in violent relationships are victims of systematic terrorism; that is, they experience multiple forms of abuse and control at the hands of their partners. Future research should focus on the extent to which violence perpetrated against women by intimate partners consists of systematic terrorism and the consequences of this type of victimization.

7. America's medical community should receive comprehensive training about the medical needs of victims of intimate partner rape and physical assault. The injury and medical utilization data generated from the NVAW Survey provide persuasive evidence of the physical and social costs associated with intimate partner violence. The survey found that in more than one-third of all rapes and physical assaults committed against women by intimates, the victim sustains an injury. Furthermore, in approximately one-third of all such injury victimizations, the victim receives some type of medical care (e.g., paramedic care, treatment in a hospital emergency facility, dental care, or physical therapy). The survey also found that approximately one-fifth of all physical assaults committed against men by intimates result in an injury to the victim, and in one-fifth of all such injury victimizations, the victim receives some type of medical treatment. Thus, of the estimated 7.7 million rapes and physical assaults committed against women and men annually by intimate partners, approximately 2.5 million will result in an injury to the victim, and approximately 680,000 will require some type of medical treatment to the victim.

Because many female and male victims of intimate partner rape and physical assault receive multiple forms of care for the same injury victimization, medical personnel in the United States treat millions of intimate partner injury victims annually. Given the large number of injury victimizations committed against women and men by intimate partners annually and the extensive nature of medical treatment to victims of intimate partner rape and physical assault, it is imperative that medical professionals receive information about the prevalence and physical consequences of intimate partner violence and the medical needs of victims and training on how to make appropriate referrals for victims with these needs.

8. The U.S. justice system community should receive comprehensive training about the safety needs of victims of intimate partner violence. As previously noted, the NVAW Survey produced dramatic confirmation of the pervasive nature and injurious consequences of intimate partner violence. Information from the survey also shows that most intimate partner rapes, physical assaults, and stalkings go unreported to law enforcement. Given these findings, criminal justice practitioners should receive comprehensive training about the safety needs of victims and the need to conduct community outreach to encourage victims of intimate partner violence to report their victimizations to the police.